RUDY UYTENHAAK ARCHITECT

Rudy Uytenhaak *Architect*

Edited by Maarten Kloos

Architectura & Natura Press

Editor
Maarten Kloos
Text editors
Chris Gordon, Birgitte de Maar
Production
Maarten Kloos, Birgitte de Maar
Translated by
Michael O'Loughlin
Design
Typography & Other Serious Matters
Printing
Industrie, Amsterdam
Publisher
Architectura & Natura Press, Amsterdam,
in conjunction with ARCAM

ISBN 90 71570 30 4
© The authors, 1993

*Published with financial support of Stichting Bedrijfspensioenfonds
voor de Bouwnijverheid (bpf-bouw); City of Apeldoorn; Bouwbedrijf
Teerenstra bv; Gezelschap Rudy Vooruyt (Woningbouwvereniging
Eigen Haard, Nevanco Woningbouw bv, Onze Woning,
Woonstichting De Doelen, Stichting Lieven de Key, Grootel's
Bouwmaatschappij bv, Bouw- en Woningdienst Amsterdam, Smit's
Bouwbedrijf bv, Sikking Aannemingsmaatschappij bv);
Stimuleringsfonds voor Architectuur*

CONTENTS

CONTENTS

INTRODUCTION

In designing the Cultural Centre in Apeldoorn Rudy Uytenhaak was confronted with an inner-city situation in which two directions are explicitly present. Typically, he did not choose one of the two, but recognized the value of both and sought the architectural quality in the spatial junction thus created. The complexity found here was not compromised, but given form and thus explained. This is how Uytenhaak is constantly attempting to build a bridge between form and meaning.

The desire to relate these concepts to each other is also literally expressed in his most important text, the inaugural lecture he gave in 1991 as professor at the Technical University in Eindhoven. It is an inspired profession of faith in which he expresses what architecture is for him and describes the 'synthesizing quality of buildings', the orchestration that gives all the aspects of the building their specific place in the score.

In developing these ideas there are again two considerations on which everything is based. Firstly, continued urbanization means that society is inevitably becoming more concentrated; and, secondly, contemporary technology makes it increasingly easier to realize 'a greater dynamism between complexity and coherence'. It is in the linking of two notions that the essence of Uytenhaak's architecture can be found. The search for 'suitable forms and organizations ... for an increasingly pluriform and dynamic society' leads him to attempt to secure 'a high degree of relaxed density'. The density of the city is interpreted as a density of values that require space, that require density and transparency to go hand-in-hand, and a form of complexity in which spaces are maximally differentiated and yet simultaneously integrated into the whole of which they are a part.

Uytenhaak's architecture has always been one great visualization of the most complex layering possible. As early as the house in Zwolle (1985) it seems as if elementary parts like the load-bearing structure and the access are first detached and then related to each other again. Also important in this respect were his 1981 counter-proposals for the Amsterdam Stadhuis/Muziektheater: he divided the large complex into parts which were then joined to each other and to the city by a subtle manipulation of street patterns and building lines.

Each of his projects reveals a conscientious quest for the right dimensions and means, for the right options available to the architect. In his own words, designing is 'the revelation of possibilities and criteria'.

MAARTEN KLOOS

THE CITY ON YOUR SKIN

Uytenhaak's research into the fine promises of modern architecture · *The city on your skin – that should be something like the sun and the wind on your skin, flashes and shadows on the retina, rustling and hissing on the eardrum, whiffs in your nose, a tingling sensation on your cheek. Modern architecture wanted to end every form of constriction. The city had to be clear. However, in its will to overpower chaos, it often placed itself outside the existing city. While it wanted to abolish hutches, it sought refuge in blocks. The façades remained mute, as if there were no longer any interesting statement to be made at the interface of building and city. Its utopias portrayed nothing but an abstract order. Rudy Uytenhaak, in search of the sometimes betrayed, sometimes unfulfilled promises of the moderns, cleans up the clogged relationship between façade and floor plan.*

Gijs Wallis de Vries discussed this with him and used fragments of this discussion, with its theses, parentheses, detours and lines of thought spun out until they break, in the following letter.[1]

To Rudy

Just as music consists of sound, a poem of letters, a painting of paint and a sculpture of material, architecture, you say, consists of space. The desire embodied by architecture, which architecture expresses, which the inhabitant enjoys and the critic perceives, is the desire for space. Which space do you desire? Are you still looking, like the moderns, for that light, transparent, limitless open *fluidum* which was described in physics long ago? Are you still shy of the imposing, heavy, opaque, closed monumental, rejecting it as oppressive, overbearing, bourgeois? Do you feel the desire for space, modern at the time, has been betrayed, that you should link up again with the desire that inspired Duiker and Mies van der Rohe and which still lives on, yes, but often so exhaustedly, so heartlessly? The desire for the 'modern' space is awash in a world of images and signs that stem from the heroic period of the modern avant-garde. Tight, smooth, preferably seamless, perfectly formed, this virtual architecture has become a plastic instead of a tectonic art. It has kept its affinity with music, but what it has in common with it is no longer the proportion but the rhythm. Just like Oud wanted it – no more façades cut out according to a pattern, but instead a rhythmic street wall and the city a single pulsating body. Nevertheless, there is no city where this has been realized. And that is no coincidence.

You do not continue along the course modernism took; you take a step backwards. You go to the source of modernism, where space still flowed as a dream image, and you draw from it a dual concept of the desire for space. Firstly, the space between the planes, pure depth, height, emptiness, the *fluidum* connected to the idea of space propagated in this century (which was originally Newtonian or Cartesian); and secondly, the space of the plane itself, its naked surface stripped of ornament, with its shallow, but sensitive fullness and thickness, its texture. If, in our imagination, the first space stimulates the sense of floating, fleeing, dissolving in a distant lightness, which always, however, symbolizes the cardinal centrality of the self, the second space symbolizes skin, body, gaze, glimpse, and the pupil more than the iris, the eyelashes more than the eye, more than the naked self the grace of the Other who keeps his aura, even from nearby. The second desire is superficial; not being drawn by depth (except as illusion), it follows shine and shadow, curve and fall, cut and fold, in order to measure on the skin both the heart and the soul. It is no coincidence that your planes are ascribed something biological (membranes, tissues, fins, scales, shells) and are increasingly less clad (no veils) – or else this cladding has grown with it, it really is a skin. In the case of the Droogbak housing you speak of 'noise barrier fins'. 'The whiff of the plane', you say tenderly.

You see the plane not merely as the boundary of space, and therefore space not simply as a *fluidum* between planes. You are interested in the depth of the plane, an idea which was already around,[2] but one I find irresistible, especially in the way it is used by you. To my mind, this should be accompanied by a critique of the one-eyed perspective, with its fixed vanishing points, and praise for cubistic or rather textural ways of seeing (if you want to exclude the volume in favour of the skin). Praise of the shallow, which like a clear stream reveals, reflects, interprets both something of its own bottom (sand, pebbles), of the sky (trees, clouds), and of its own flow (fish, plants). You realize the 'shallow depth' and 'phenomenal transparency' of Colin Rowe and Robert Slutzky.[3] What you have in common with Rowe is that you are looking for a grammar, a syntax. Where you probably differ from him is in your preference for an oblique, tangential, sideways, angular view. It is less a matter of the axis (as in Rowe) as of the rotation (your *palazzi* in the Czaar Peterbuurt). In this the geometry is a little altered, even though you do not go so far as to pleat and fold. It is more a matter of cutting. Each threshold, frame, ledge, edge, sill, seam or plinth matters. 'The whiff of the plane.'

In the formation of the plane, light and dark are preferred to the colours of the rainbow. And when you work with colour, it is to acquire tonality, not a primary colour and certainly not a symbolic colour. The principle of mascara, shadowy set back and light brought forward. Colours must not refer, but seduce. But you do not go so far as to include a vase of flowers in your designs. That is for the resident or visitor to do. And for the façade, where you go further, the expectation aroused must be tempered: nothing more than an invitation proffered.

Views of the City · For you the crucial point seems to be the façade. The façade controls the relationship between house and street, between the intimate and the public. For this you apply the space of the plane already discussed. I wonder how this space is related to the ground level. Has architecture been removed from its cradle, its place, and become a mobile object? Indeed, it is also the vehicle of our dreams. In reality this vehicle has come to a permanent halt and thus 'petrified'; it has itself been turned into a place. The rapture is the enchantment which exists thanks to the *genius loci*. Nevertheless the

Droogbak

intimacy of the interior, and equally the openness of the exterior, is not created by the façade. You seem to be in some doubt as to whether a façade forms an exterior or an interior, but you know better. Urban life can not be captured by façades, even though the façades lend a face to the city. The interior too is a world independent of the façade, although this façade frames the light coming from the outside world.

There is something else involved apart from the façade, which has nothing to do with the private and the public but with the increasing density of city and landscape. Which element, which architectural principle do you use for this? For you, every building must be a unity *in* the city but at the same time create a unity *of* the city. You borrow something from Le Corbusier's *unités* or Mies's *centres* but temper their detachment. And you derive a certain hierarchy from the blocks of Berlage or Otto Wagner, but you make it looser (as in the 'restoration' of the original order of canal and radial in the Weesperstraat development). You want to create new spaces by making old spaces denser. A fine example is the Uffizi complex, in which Vasari introduced three classical types (the forum, the amphitheatre and the triumphal gate) into the medieval morphology of Florence, dissecting and changing them and creating at the same time a new relationship between the city (with its original Roman pattern) and the river Arno. The element that plays a decisive role here is the plan – with the plan one can trace the increased density, with the plan one simultaneously organizes an interior and an exterior.

The growing density of the crowded country · If 'space' still has any importance in an age dominated by space-devouring media and transport, then it is because of the question of territorial density. Your approach is syntactic, with a metaphoric allusion. 'Condensing space',[4] according to the title of the lecture you gave when you took up the chair of architectural and town-planning design at the Technical University in Eind-hoven.[5]

Living in the city was usually thought unattractive by society's upper circles, whether they were capitalist or socialist. The move to the suburbs by those who had money or power did not, however, take place every-where. In Vienna, the most desired residential location was (and is) the centre, followed by the 'Ring', and only then the suburbs, where there were hardly any villa parks.[6] High density meant 'quality' in all respects.

Density as a quality is not the density of a single func-tion. Nor is it a density of a single design. Density is also the condensed history of a place. Density is not a physical but a cultural fact. You rightly believe that for high den-sity you must not only seek a suitable morphology and typology but also think of the investment density, which is not just an economic question but also one of civiliza-tion. Who lives there, how much can they spend on their dwelling, what will they do with the surroundings? Neglected neighbourhoods become attractive again when artists, businessmen and academics go to live there. The substance was almost written off, but culture is invested in. This 'liberal' urban renewal depends on the type of dwelling (flexibility of the structure, attractive-ness of the style and the charm of the ornamentation), but the neighbourhood is also important (location near a park, public facilities, main roads, shops, station and schools). In 'socialist' urban renewal the suburbs and the standards laid down there are the only things looked at.

The urban renewal promoted by the state has been accompanied by a reduction in population density. Why did the lowering of dwelling occupation, which was taking place independent of the policy of the authorities, not lead to attempts to increase the number of dwellings per hectare? And why did the reduction in population density differ per neighbourhood? For example, in the Kinkerbuurt (a neighbourhood in Amsterdam) the number of dwellings declined from 200 to 50 per hectare, and in the Pijp, not far from there, from 200 to 150. In the Kinkerbuurt there was much demolition, the new buildings there are lower in height than those they replaced and there is now much parking space and greenery; even so it looks miserable. In the Pijp there was little demolition, much renovation, there is not very much greenery and the parking problem remains, but the Pijp is pleasant. In both neighbourhoods then, high density was seen as undesirable: it was not the neglect of the area but the housing density that was blamed for the neighbourhoods' poor image. People despised the narrow streets (though in fact they were less narrow than those in some 1970s' residential precincts, the Dutch *woonerven*), the cramped dwellings (though they had higher ceilings than your standard modern dwelling), and the messy areas inside the blocks (though they were less confined than in the suburbs). The criteria of the suburbs, with their unrestricted green space and parking facilities, were blindly applied. But while these criteria were strictly adhered to in the Kinkerbuurt, in the Pijp they were applied more flexibly. The needs were recognized but the quantity was determined only in the context of the area, while looking for a concrete place and characteristic form. So, not quantity but quality. Yet quantity is important for you,

Weesperstraat

not as a 'right', not to make everything equal, which is unrealistic and doomed to failure, but to weigh up things against each other, and to argue for compensation. Density is an architectural criterion for using land intensively. You have come through your baptism of fire as an architect working mainly in 'socialistic' urban renewal by shaking off ideology and committing yourself to a disciplined approach.[7]

Cubistic eros · It is time for a new relationship between both house and street, city and landscape, a relationship which combats the polluting, choking and fragmenting use of space. With regard to the landscape, modern architecture has allowed itself to be pushed completely on to the defensive: architecture is alleged to pollute the horizon, it is said that it is not regional, that it is much too rational to respect the *genius loci*. Modern architecture, they say, is too one-dimensional.

Descendant of cubism, it should once again learn a lesson from Picasso in how you combine layers and discontinuities, constant movement and sensitive viewpoints (the advice of Hockney, the optimist). The pleasure of going around, the desire to go along and through the planes, curves, folds and cuts, to touch, to stroke and to kiss, to glide and sway, and then to roam, lost for a moment in a field, resting on a line, floating on a point. 'Parcourir à loisir ses magnifiques formes.'[8]

Layering is not just a question of density but also of poetic freedom. No more lamenting the scarcity of space. The Netherlands is not full. Yes, the country is certainly becoming fuller, but take the pressure off. Smart density is the motto. 'Condensing space', is what is crucial. The space must be used at least twice, or three times, four times, eight times. No increase in density without a decrease in density: concentration here, thinning out there. There is a desire for emptiness, emptiness between, in and around the fullness. Since we, unlike Rietveld, no longer think of the designed space as something separated from the general, natural space, but as something to be added to the cultural space and its artificial horizon, we must recognize the danger of congestion which appears when things are added without limit and we must be careful with materials, places and characters. Let us carry new spaces into the existing space and ensure they prosper repeatedly and meaningfully in high densities. Such densities could nevertheless clash with your predilection for transparency. That's why you say this must be understood figuratively, phenomenally, and conceptually rather than literally. Literal transparency would surrender the space (to the looming chaos) instead of gaining space (for the promised happiness). The same applies, according to you, to density: dense transparency (which is not like an aquarium) and transparent density (which does not restrain). To my mind, that is a plea for opacity. Is modern architecture capable of the paradox of opaque transparency or the chiasmus of transparency and density? It set in motion something that has not yet been realized. You are in the process of showing that.

Style

The syntactic arrangement of points, lines and layers is metonymic, a release of a tautological nature: as if the desire for architecture were a desire for space, and architecture consisted of space, and expressed space. As if ultimately you only learn grammatical models. There is also a metaphorical dimension to increased density, a release of contents. The metaphor is the smallest allegory, the densest myth, the shortest story.[9] Increased density is also a stacking and mixing of a communicative nature: the arrangement of references, manifestations, meanings and expressions which space can bear. Density is the metonymy for the entire space of existence, yet that space can only be realized when, simultaneously, the metaphors of existence are constructed in the mind.

Spiritualized craftsmanship · All architectural design processes proceed along two lines: on the one hand the defining of the programme (goal, desire, requirement, content); on the other hand the defining of space (form, order, structure, expression). You analyse the programme until it is capable of being manipulated. This is in fact a revision of the modern, because the forms no longer want to follow the functions. In order to be able to manipulate the functions you practice a sort of constructivism, you look for the synthesis, the integration.

In your research into the unfulfilled promise of modern architecture you quote Rietveld, Le Corbusier, and Mies. But how modern can a 'classic' be, how classical a modernist? Don't you become a classicist yourself by making classics of the moderns of the past?[10] Just as Wittkower searched for the principles of Renaissance architecture,[11] you look for the principles of modern architecture. You make it equally autonomous. The question of the autonomy of architecture, formulated since Rossi's *Architecture of the City* as a question of typology and morphology, is for you inextricably bound up with the need for character. For you, character is the giving of a value to a form. It is what is currently called quality, or allure, or cachet. I think it also evokes the demand for style. Style is the manner of explicitly expressing whatever character. Style is at stake, an approach recently made fun of (and challenged) by that crooked formula of Koolhaas: 'a house with no style'. The danger of style is that it becomes a trade mark and always falls back on the same thing. But real style is in the unparalleled presence. Autonomy through semantic absence and characteristic presence, which can only be in the material.

Your touchstone is not the contents but the form. Craftsmanship is mastery, but also modesty, reliability, respectability (as Tessenow appreciated). Yet you want 'enthusiastic craftsmanship'. Enthusiasm is the attribute of the romantic loner, the creative artist, the struggling spirit. For you modernity is not a history (revolution, ideology), nor even a temporal perspective (because the future it believes itself to possess has been betrayed, the liberation from hutches has become a dictatorship of small blocks). Modernity is a timeless quality. The eternal promise of modernity is a growing culture, advancing awareness. Not a utopia but a project,[12] you call it a 'Faustian' project, in which it is a question of growing habitability, turning the world into culture and the development of the language which our consciousness formulates from it. Consciousness of progress. In fact, you deny the rough, raw primitiveness that pursues architecture as its origins as much as the extreme, the mechanical or the electronic that haunts it like its apocalypse. You pin your hopes on the subtle, civilized, aesthetic – in use too. And, indeed, according to Stendhal, beauty is nothing else but a promise of happiness.[13] Your optimism does not aim at a distant ideal, but a nearby space, that of the growing habitability of the earth.

Is there then nothing to be said for the architecture of representation – the non-affected representation, as practised by a Vandenhove? There is surely more to it than a reference to bourgeois culture (in the sense of good manners)? Neo-classicism does not stand for bourgeois alone; you can find it from Calcutta to Chicago, from Shanghai to Helsinki and wasn't ancient Rome itself a melting pot?

Whereas the classics were in search of meaning (a column was not a column but represented something, rural or civilized, male or female, girlish or gigantic), the moderns are looking for themselves (now a column wants to be a column). The expressive order has become a tautological one: the confirmation of identity rather than the riddle of the sphinx. However, you simply reject the self-referential logic of the obstructive presence as such (or in the name of an ideology). You present the 'presence of the building as building' as a form of modesty. The presence is not the image, nor the ideology, nor the technology. The presence of the building derives from the type, the spot and the character. Presence requires style, the way of making character expressive, of making the spot present and the type useful. You think, for example, that the danger with the Dutch structuralists is that space acquires no character but becomes an endless intermediary space with a false topography, and a poorly defined function. You note the lack of hierarchy and the flourishing of ambiguities.[14] You have turned your back on these ambiguities.

Language

Architects like to speak of reading buildings, but by this they mean something other than the reading of books or

Nieuw Sloten

maps. Whoever reads a book does not read letters, nor even words, although he has to read what is written. Language is not about letters or words. 'Just read, what's there is not there.'[15] Language attributes something to reality which is evoked, described, interpreted as state, sensation, idea or event. In language, meaning, negative or positive, is ascribed to the reality we encounter. No matter how much it affects us, reality is in itself meaning-less and only acquires the attribute 'meaning' thanks to language (and language only acquires the attribute 'event' thanks to reality).[16] The event which happens to architecture is use. You want to invite a use by enticing it with readable forms. That use is not random and the form is not free. The beautiful form prepares the beauti-ful use, to quote Taut freely.[17]

Dream image · An architect's dreams have a life. His dreams change that life, all too often because they find that the existing is just deficient; therefore they correct it and thus give it a negative connotation. The danger in designing is constantly seeing deficiencies and obs-tacles. Dreams can also reinforce the existing in its exis-tence, enjoy its values and honour it in its traditions (the promise of designing is to celebrate the city). The goals of modern architecture were originally often negatively for-mulated (modern architecture felt weighed down by the old things, it wanted a major 'clean-up'). Reconstruction, in fact a glorification of bombardment, became its alibi. It forgot its goals and was absorbed by means (technology, legislation).

In your dream of a building the erotic is a vital vector, but also something of a more infinite character, some-thing that postpones the embrace, a cosmic or even theo-

logical vector (an exaltation which again is very sensible:
'God is in the detail'). Whatever the case may be, as soon
as one steps outside the spatial it is not easy to say what
architecture means. You repeat that space is the reality
for the architect (as the paint is for the painter, the word
for the poet, the sound for the composer). This tautology
makes it possible for you to fall back on grammar, syntax
– it seems principled but is in fact provisional. In order to
be able to carry meaning the form has to listen to the rules
which define it, you say. That sounds like de Saussure's
structuralist idea of language, that it is the formal differences which make language, minimal differences which
give signs a value. And, just like de Saussure, you conclude 'The game then follows on naturally'. Structural-
ism teaches that through the formal differences the parts
refer to wholes. You mean metonymy. I wonder how you
escape from arbitrariness, except by accepting 'convention' or 'tradition', which only means a displacement of
the question: because to what extent do you have to stick
to convention, and what inspiration can be found in tradition beyond that of an obligation to form and syntax.

Now one could say that the entire problem does not
apply to architecture, because, after all, it is not a language since you can not translate it (like you can Dutch
into English). The question of the motivation of architecture is in fact always easy to answer: it is the programme,
the function, the technology, or the quality. Nevertheless,
an architecture motivated in that way has led to blocks,
boxes, semantic voids which can then be 'arbitrarily'
divided up and disseminated instead of being playfully
narrated, translated, declined. That declension is still
purely syntactic, but the narration is not – while the
translation is surely no longer a translation of a pro-

gramme? Translation here refers to the exchange of linguistic treasures: stories, sayings, puns, poems and myths, which deal with forms of architecture and which pass these on to those who understand the language.

Condensed space, dense language · The question of syntax and grammar is of primary importance in 'reading' the 'condensed' space. The composition of point, line and plane into space, and its complexity, its layers. One thinks of Mies or of Dutch still lifes. Reading is then an assault on seeing: captured by the splendour, grasped by the vanity. Reading is a mental ecstasy: the comprehension of objective signs, subjective emotions and conceptual meanings, and furthermore of the significance expressed in signs. How could we otherwise recognize spaces like gateway, street, bridge, lock, column, wall, screen, door or window? When you say that you make spaces which refer to nothing, that your architecture should only be about space (and a poem about letters, a painting about paint, a song about sound) then there would appear to be no other field to which architecture is related (no more God, but no man either, no more sky, but no earth either, no more death, and therefore no life either). There is only reading as 'scanning' of space. When you want to make a difference between private and public, or between the interior and the exterior worlds, those are not merely spatial questions. You are also talking about meaning then. The tautology is only apparent. What you mean by 'listening' is actually less a command (listening to rules) than an appeal to wisdom (listening to the 'meaning' of rules).

I imagine that the naïve reading of content can be related to an acutely literal reading, the symbolism of grammar itself, rather as Mallarmé developed it.[18] No fear of semantic banality, pleasure in syntactic opacity, a desire to invite metaphors by playing with syntax. I also think of the loss and recovery of 'grace' which von Kleist wrote about in 1801: the youthful innocence and grace that man loses through an excess of self-consciousness can be recovered, while contemplating the enchanting, 'eccentric' mechanical movements of marionettes.[19] He can only conquer his woodenness by describing an ellipse around his subjectivity. This 'eccentric course' is neither literal nor figurative. It is a mental figure.

Celebrations of the modern · Your primacy of grammar is undoubtedly mental. If reading is mental it is a question of reading what is disclosed to perception and seeing what is revealed to thought. The *noèteon* (or concept), that which must be thought, is inextricably bound up with the way in which the *aisthèteon*, that which you can only perceive with the senses, affects you and how it changes your percept.[20] After all, it is not only a matter of understanding (that your design dramatizes a concept by expressing it in space), but also of emotion (that your design interprets an emotion by enlarging it). Only in this way can you rise above the brief (whoever the client is) and escape fashion and clichés.

Language, no matter how literally we understand it, always lives from translation. Translation as the putting into words of feelings, ideas and things, as the bringing over from one language to another, as the declension and conjugation of signs or as the attribution of meaning. Language is only purely syntactic, grammatical, in so far as its effect, propagated in the metonymic axis, can name an area of freedom and constantly revolves around the metaphoric, paradigmatic axis in a space of politics (pronouncing the rules which are obeyed), of eroticism (expressing what is desired), and finally of the poetic (speaking the ineffable, which makes language turn back along the metonymic axis). It is then not just a question of recognizing the signs (which is no more than an acknowledgement of the power of the dictionary), but of researching the hallucinatory field of forces, the modern urban *fluidum* in which everything dissolves and in which only the fragment has a grammar. This research is terribly complex but does not necessarily have to be deconstructivist. With you, on the contrary, it is constructivist in its contents and formalist in its expression. Thanks to planes, it makes legible spaces that are extremely layered and dense and also ordered. The plane, on the one hand, is metonymic: it stands for a whole (the city, or the continuity of space). On the other hand, it is metaphoric: it stands for an idea, a culture, a promise (happiness, or the continuity of life). Just as pupils are metonymic for the face, the entire body, and metaphoric for the soul, the entire person, the architecturally composed plane refers to absences by making them present in the form of space.

Rotate the metaphoric axis back to the metonymic plane and hail the meaning released. The delirious space: you could say that every celebration of modern architecture is actually the 'release' of the desire for space. The required inventiveness for this was liberated by the first moderns, whom we shouldn't really hold to the sometimes simple slogans they made, such as Mies's 'Less is more', Mart Stam's 'A nut is hexagonal and everyone knows why', or Hannes Meyer's 'Paint is only there to protect the steel'. These were statements against the grain, surly or bad-tempered, angrily or petulantly flung

*Czaar
Peterbuurt*
(Palazzo)

at moaning pedants, but they were also somewhat child-ish. According to you, modernism actually promised something very different than the exhaustively preached sobriety, even if, as Rietveld once said, there is an unsus-pected luxury hidden in sobriety. Luxury that modernism should have, the luxury of restrained wealth.[21]

What inspires architecture?

During the course of our discussions, which started some time ago, we clarified our respective positions on four or five central questions. Let me just summarize them and try to formulate a conclusion.

What is the use of the old moderns? How modern can a 'classic' be and how classical can a modern architect be? What interests you is catching the inventiveness released in the works left to us. You combat the danger of a watered-down tradition by looking for what this creative freedom entails. Freedom in what, from what and for what? The answers follow below.

Immediately after the historical question of the mod-ern tradition comes the ontological question: what is the essence of architecture? You are concerned with space, the space between the planes (like a modern 'classic') and the space in or of the plane itself ('the whiff of the plane'). This means freedom in space by celebrating the desire and meeting the need. The third question concerns the design process. The design that invents space follows two lines, on the one hand the definition of the programme, where you make, in a constructivist sense, the contents manipulable; on the other hand, the definition of the expression, where you formalize type, place and charac-ter. It is a stylistic question. Your style is not classicist (although you are looking for the moderns' rules). Unlike Wittkower or Rowe, for example, who reduce architecture to principles, form to mathematics, while keeping the content general and so distilling a genuine classicism from their material, you are more like a mannerist. That is, you approach expression formalistically in order to free it from over-general contents and to make it available for very special ones. After all, formalism is not so much formal as strong. In this way you avoid the subjective as well as the ideological. Classicism plus formalism is mannerism. Mannerism, for its part, is not so much 'mannered' as strategic, a struggle against classicism (with its humanistic constants and universals), but it also erects a barrier against the baroque (with its cosmic ecstasies and harmonies). Your formalism is therefore not formal but experimental (a struggle against over-subjective forms of expression as much as against over-general contents). Furthermore, for you mannerism is less a critique of stagnation than a promise of freedom, free of obsessive or overwhelming forms.

The fourth question concerns making the space legible, the reading and writing of space, the language of architecture. Is architecture about nothing else but space? In your work there are enough twists and turns that imply something else, despite a modest emphasis on form. It is even the challenge to track them down, those bodily, biological references of the façade (the skin, the iris of the building), those historical, even mythical, references of the plan (the layers, the density of the city). But you keep them in suspense, not a utopia but a project. This means the freedom to welcome content.

The fifth question concerns the practice of the architect. How do you fight against economies, how do you profit from deregulation, how do you play along with the market? Without going systematically into these questions, I would conclude that your most important response, as revealed by your approach to space, your style and your statements, is to condense space. To increase the density at some points in order to reduce it elsewhere for the benefit of the whole; that is the slogan of your work but also what makes your work efficient. The space-in-the-plane gives meaningful space to what the floor-plan-in-layers casually carries into the chaos of the city: the osmosis of interior or exterior.

Finally, I would like to raise a few questions concerning the teaching, research and criticism of modern architecture. Whoever takes your work to heart will teach modernism not as a 'schoolmaster' but as a 'master'.[22] A paradox which is typical of an existential philosophy of teaching: the good teacher does not reach his student, the good student excels his teacher. Perhaps the only way to comprehend this paradox completely is to first teach a modern 'doctrine' (with eternal principles and a general content). Yes, and as far as research is concerned, if you do not want to research the 'principles' or 'mathematics' of an 'ideal' modernism but the modalities and ways of expression of specific, historically determined monuments and writings, and nevertheless maintain a universal ideal, then it is a good idea to decline and conjugate the simply inevitable (modern) classicism into a (modern) mannerism. With regard to criticism, the question is whether it still has any point, and whether it is not more a question of a creative discussion about what inspires architecture, and what there is to see and think about.

GIJS WALLIS DE VRIES

NOTES

1. Most of this dialogue took place in the winter of 1992-93.

2. Gilles Deleuze, *Logique du sens*, Paris 1969. The blurb reads: 'le plus profond c'est la peau'.

3. Colin Rowe and Robert Slutzky, *Transparency: Literal and Phenomenal, Perspecta*, Basle, Boston, Berlin 1963.

4. Translator's note: the Dutch title *Ruimte dichten* may also be a pun on 'Poeticizing Space'.

5. Rudy Uytenhaak, *Ruimte dichten. Opdracht, visie en passie*. Inaugural lecture, 15 February 1991, Technische Universiteit Eindhoven.

6. Donald Olsen, *The city as a work of art*, New Haven and London 1986. The nice thing about an analysis like Olsen's is his unabashed preference for the monumental, the ornate, spectacular, and above all, the luxurious, enjoyment and pleasure. Dimensions which were missing from urban renewal.

7. Rudy Uytenhaak, 'Vormgeven aan een karakteristiek', *Forum* no. 4 1984, pp. 42-45.

8. Charles Baudelaire, *La géante, Les fleurs du Mal*, 1861.

9. Gianbattista Vico, *La Scienza Nuova* [1744], ed. P. Rossi, Milan 1977; Libro secondo, II, 'Della logica poetica', 2: 'talché ogni metafora (...) vien ad essere una piccola favoletta'.

10. You yourself have formulated the problem as the paradox of the creative tradition. See *Forum* no. 6 1977.

11. Rudolph Wittkower, *Architectural Principles in the Age of Humanism*, London (1949) 1988.

12. Linked in a way different from that in M. Tafuri, *Progetto e Utopia*, Rome 1973.

13. Stendhal, *Rome, Naples et Florence*, Paris 1826, ed. P. Brunel, 1987, p. 57. 'La beauté n'est jamais, ce me semble, qu'une promesse de bonheur.' A variation on the statement from *De l'amour*: 'La beauté n'est que la promesse du bonheur.' (chap. XVII).

14. Rudy Uytenhaak, *Ruimte dichten*. 'The experiment made in the Dapper neighbourhood with the "street garden" shows that insufficient awareness in making the differing quality of street and garden in a closed-block structure leads to the failure of the apparent enlargement of the environment. The architects involved, a number of whom have a "structuralist" background, are looking – on the basis of their ideas for an attached dwelling around a portico – for a more diffuse order with spatial forms that dissolve into "transitions". In this sense it seems as if the experiments with structures and links, which led to the creation of various types of exterior spaces, have brought about a fudging of norms with regard to the quality of those spaces.' (p. 45)

15. M. Nijhoff, *Awater*, 1934.

16. On the conspiracy of event and meaning, see Gilles Deleuze, *Logique du sens*.

17. Rudy Uytenhaak, *Forum* no. 6 1977.

18. Jacques Scherer, *Grammaire de Mallarmé*, Paris 1977. See also Philippe Sollers, *L'écriture et l'expérience des limites, Littérature et totalité*, Paris 1968.

19. '... so findet sich auch, wenn die Erkenntnis gleichsam durch ein Unendliches gegangen ist, die Grazie wieder ein; so, dass sie, zu gleicher Zeit, in demjenigen menschlichen Körperbau am reinsten erscheint, der entweder gar keins, oder ein unendliches Bewusstsein hat, d.h. in dem Gliedermann, oder in dem Gott', Heinrich von Kleist, *Über das Marionettentheater*, (1801) Jena 1920, pp. 15-16.

20. For concept, affect and percept, see Gilles Deleuze and Félix Guattari, *Qu'est-ce que la philosophie*, Paris 1991; and for the *noèteon* and the *aisthèteon*, Gilles Deleuze, *Différence et Répétition*, Paris 1969, Book III, 'L'image de la pensée', pp. 182 ff.

21. Baudelaire has already ascribed it to our country: 'Là tout n'est qu'ordre et beauté, luxe, calme et volupté' (*L'invitation au Voyage*).

22. According to Hans van Dijk, 'Onderwijzersmodernisme, van inspiratiebron tot ballast: de moderne traditie in Nederland', *Archis* 6 1990, pp. 8-13.

URBAN RENEWAL

A nose doesn't define a face, nor a statement a building. Light, dimensions and material make space concrete and lend it character. The design discovers relationships between programme and site, opens both as spatial identities and thus introduces them into culture. Spaces of value – architecture reflects culture in its own unique way.

Ten plans, ten sites, ten forms that do not simply follow functions but in which the formal structure follows an analysis of programmatic and situational desires. The reading of a situation's characteristics is activated in the light of a programme, the situation offers starting points for defining a building type and conjugating it.

RUDY UYTENHAAK

*Czaar
Peterstraat*

Urban plans and study for Czaar Peterbuurt, Amsterdam
commissioned by: Comité Behoud en Herstel and others
designed: 1980-92

95 dwellings and 4 offices, Czaar Peterstraat, 141 dwellings,
Conradstraat, design for 27 dwellings
with: Marco Romano, Harry Pappot, Kees Stoffels
commissioned by: Woningbouwvereniging Eigen Haard
designed: 1985-93
realized by: Grootel's Bouwmaatschappij bv 1990-93

The series of projects for the Czaar Peterbuurt attempts to renew this
neighbourhood on the basis of its existing characteristics. The first plan
aims at the preservation and renovation of the existing buildings by pro-
posing new infills for the gaps in the area, while for the urban spaces
improvements are proposed for lightening this neighbourhood, the
most densely built in the Netherlands. The plan for Oostenburg proposes a park in the continuation of the waterway, surrounded by semi-
open buildings. This half-open building type is later developed into
palazzi as a synthesis between strip building and blocks, suggesting that

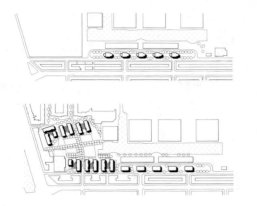

*First plan
Czaar
Peterbuurt*

*Plan for
Oostenburg*

two strips form a single building in the public space. The shell of the
building is formed by the overhanging roof and the formal sturdy walls,
the 'inner' court is a space with layered construction of a more informal
and light character.

The design for the block along Czaar Peterstraat continues the urban
fabric of the Czaar Peterbuurt by filling in the original site, which is only
twenty-four metres deep, as much as possible as a single block. An
oppressive interior for the block is avoided by making four separate
'towers' to the west. However, to avoid fragmenting the street wall here,
these towers appear to be joined by the balconies, the cornice and the
balustrades to produce a single wall.

A continuous balcony has been made on Czaar Peterstraat on the
third floor, so that the balconies are included as unobtrusively as possible in the street façade and a cornice is created that will, above all,
become part of the profile of the street. That also happens in the lower
part of the building; the relief of the balustrade and the different glass
fronts are variations on a theme typical of the area.

The urban plan study applies this experience to formulate a broader
perspective for the Czaar Peterbuurt; the evolution of a characteristic
street neighbourhood.

Palazzi

Situation

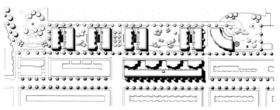

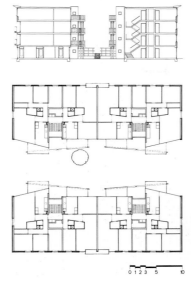

*Cross-section
Palazzi*

*Typical floor-
plan*

*Ground-floor
plan*

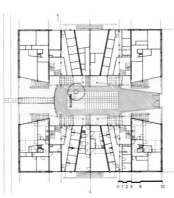

Ground-floor plan, Czaar Peterstraat

Third-floor plan, Czaar Peterstraat

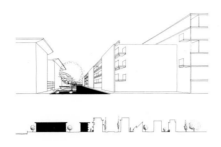

Street profiles

Urban plans Weesperstraat, Amsterdam
commissioned by: Buurtcomité Weesperbuurt, Munic
designed: 1980-86

Design for two office buildings, Weesperstraat, 205 dwellings,
2 shops, 15 offices, lunchroom and parking, Weesperstraat/
Nieuwe Kerkstraat, design for 56 dwellings and parking,
Lepelstraat/Weesperstraat
with: Tiemen Koetsier, Felix Claus, Kees Kaan, John Bosch,
Joost Hovenier, Gé van Dam
commissioned by: M.A.B., Onze Woning
designed: 1986-88
realized by: Smit's Bouwbedrijf, 1992

The successive plans for Weesperstraat, which dissects the concentric
rings of Amsterdam's principal canals, attempt to solve the encounter of
a historically rich structure with the rough scale imposed by the construction of the underground system and the development of
Weesperstraat as a major traffic route. This traffic radial denying the
rings of canals instead of ceding priority to the canals at the junctions.

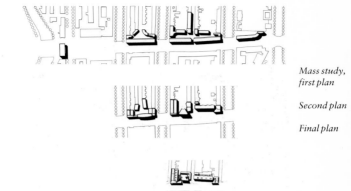

Mass study, first plan

Second plan

Final plan

The first plan includes a double row of housing with a residential court in between. The plan was rejected, however, because it did not conform to noise legislation. The second plan emphasizes housing along the canals, while offices on a more metropolitan scale are envisaged in Weesperstraat. In the realized plan the functions are to a large extent separated; the office tower has been replaced by a block of flats set back somewhat to escape the noise of the traffic.

The accent is placed on the canals by drawing on the principles of Amsterdam's canal façades with regard to proportion and form. But to avoid the canals, when perceived from the traffic artery, giving the impression of a miniature city, buildings of a significantly larger scale are included in the perspective of Weesperstraat and, at the same time, integrated into the dense urban fabric of the inner city.

The architecture of the realized plan is therefore not an architecture of blocks but one of planes. By researching for every façade the urban space to which it reacts, a strong differentiation is created for each plane.

For instance, the quality of the urban space of the canals is formally supported by the architecture of the canal houses. The interpretation of this architecture has led to much diversity, even though characteristic

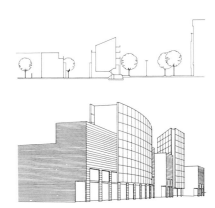

*First plan,
cross-section*

*Second plan,
office
buildings*

constants (gables and a classical proportioning of the windows) are
used. Functionally, as many canal-house dwellings as possible have
their living-room facing the canal to get light in the evenings.

In my understanding of contextual design, design freedom actually
arises from an understanding of what is characteristic of the situation.
The canal houses realized in the plan are, in terms of material and detail,
new, but in dimension and scale the familiar game with the rhythm of
the façade is being played, as usual involving the whole series of individual façades. In elaborating the architecture the element of scale was
important. Different surface qualities, and therefore different textures
of shadow and light, have been introduced in order to create an architectural dynamism.

By reacting specifically to streets and canals, a plan emerged with a
diversity of housing situations and dwelling types. Apart from 205
dwellings, the plan includes a bicycle shed, a lunchroom, 2 shops, and
15 offices, all this above a 2-storey underground car-park. In Weesperstraat there is a 12-storey rhombus-shaped tower with 4 dwellings per
floor and a 10-storey, more horizontal block. Bearing in mind the architecturally varied character of the surroundings, the architecture of the
complex has been consciously kept expressively plain.

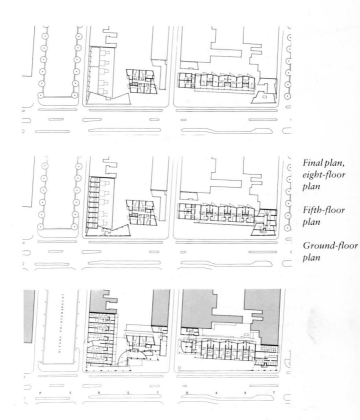

*Final plan,
eight-floor
plan*

*Fifth-floor
plan*

*Ground-floor
plan*

*Façade
Weesper-
straat, detail*

*Canal houses,
Nieuwe
Prinsengracht,
floor plans*

 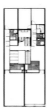 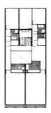  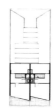

*South façade,
detail*

95 dwellings and parking, Droogbak, Amsterdam
with: Felix Claus, Gerard Kruunenberg
commissioned by: Stichting Lieven de Key
designed: 1986
realized by: Smit's Bouwbedrijf, 1989

The Droogbak housing project near Amsterdam's Central Station is located between the railway embankment and a major road on the one hand and the former harbour front, with its characteristic seventeenth-century houses, on the other. In order to avoid disturbing existing urban qualities, the new building contrasts with the urban fabric and at the same time recedes from its 'partner', a former government office building dating from the nineteenth century.

Functionally, the building serves as a noise barrier on one side and a wall of housing on the other. Thus there are two very different faces to an apartment building in which one can live in a comfortable, metropolitan manner on this apparently impossible site. The living-rooms and main bedrooms are on the quiet southern side, directed towards the inner city. The kitchens and other bedrooms on the northern side have a view of the IJ river through a noise-resistant glass screen.

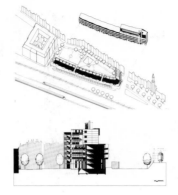

Isometric drawing

Cross-section

The analysis of the problems of the site and of the desired programme led directly to the concept of an ideal cross-section for this location. In the best tradition of public housing the types developed in this cross-section are repeated over the length of the building. The large dimensions created in this manner acquire 'scale' through varied building heights and through the autonomy of the prefabricated components in the south façade between the end walls. These brise-soleil-style balcony screens, which divide up the main form of the building into a stack consisting of two simple forms, create a spatial, spherical wall. The end walls are of brick for reasons of contrast and context and for technical reasons. The north façade reacts to the scale of the infrastructure and has a consciously large scale, built up from a series of smaller elements. Three types of acoustic screen make it an expressive façade, the upper screens moreover catching the sunlight as it reaches over the top of the building.

Ground-floor plan

Second-floor plan

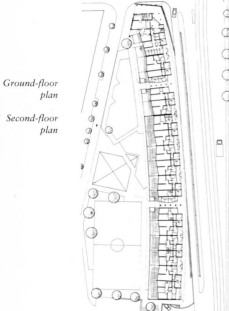

*Group
dwelling*

*South façade,
balconies*

Entrance

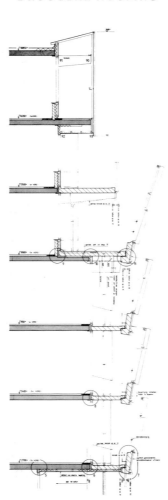

*Noise-
resistant glass
screens*

Model

Urban plan, housing and shops, Hobbemastraat, The Hague
with: S O G Z, Joanne de Jager, Joost Hovenier, Jan Peter Wingender
commissioned by: V Z O S, municipality of The Hague,
Woningbouwvereniging 's Gravenhage and others
designed: 1990
realized by: Wilma Bouw bv, 1993

Hobbemastraat, a shopping street in the urban renewal area of Schilderswijk in The Hague, is to be completely renovated. This first plan defines the rules with which successive building plans must comply. An arcade has been proposed to limit the extent to which the street has to be widened. The design dramatizes this arcade by accentuating the height of the lower part of the building. The upper part is given a concrete grid with a strong sill effect that hangs like an open lattice work slightly in front of the arcade's stainless-steel columns. For the side-streets a new interpretation has been made of the nineteenth-century type of lower maisonette (with garden) and upper maisonette (with roof terrace).

Façade with prefab concrete elements

Ground, first, second and third-floor plan

28 dwellings, Sumatraplantsoen/Tidorestraat, Amsterdam
with: Theo Peppelman, André Hoek
commissioned by: Gemeentelijk Woningbedrijf, Huib Bakker
designed: 1988
realized by: Huib Bakker, 1991

A volume, all the elements of which are located within the envelope of
the street façades, is used to complete the short side of an Amsterdam
School block.

North façade

180 dwellings Java-eiland, Amsterdam
with: Ad van Aert, Kees Stoffels
commissioned by: bpf-bouw
designed: 1993
realized by: Bouwcombinatie Java-eiland, due 1994-

Five different 'housing programmes', each in monumental buildings along both quays, individual buildings forming a classical wall.

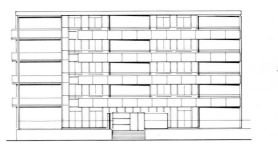

South façade

Whiff of stone

123 dwellings and parking, Koningin Wilhelminaplein, Amsterdam
with: Tiemen Koetsier, Harry Pappot, Ad van Aert, Gé van Dam
commissioned by: bpf-bouw
designed: 1989
realized by: Bouwbedrijf Teerenstra bv, 1991

In Amsterdam Nieuw-West, built thirty years ago as part of the General
Extension Plan (1935), the park-like Koningin Wilhelminaplein lies just
outside the ring. To stimulate this area socially and spatially it was
decided to increase the housing density there by adding three 'light and
luxurious' blocks of flats, 'apartments in the park'. The substantial volume of the blocks – five dwellings per floor – is softened by employing a
vertical plasticity and a strategic use of directions and sight-lines. The
impression of autonomous objects freely following their own internal
order is illusory. The motifs and discipline of the architecture have actually been developed on the basis of the floor plans and the possibility of
orienting them with regard to the context.

Parallel to the Slotervaart the blocks of flats follow the principal
direction of the area and the main road. On the park side, the façades are
at right angles to the diagonal avenue of trees across 'the square', so that

Whiff of glass

these façades do not form a plane but three coulisses providing a more transparent boundary to the park. This means that the north façades oriented to the main road also have the character of screens. Thanks to this layout four of the five dwellings on each floor have an unobstructed view of greenery and water on the south-west side and even the usually less desirable north-east dwelling protrudes so far that it catches the sun, though only late in the afternoon. The dwellings are built using tunnel formwork, a system which is financially attractive but often found to be uncompromising. In this case the tunnel is cut obliquely across the front. These open sides are closed by a simple curtain wall composed of various standard building elements and framed by red cedar posts, while the structural surfaces are clad with brick.

Special attention has been paid to the access of the dwellings. On all the upper floors the halls located in the middle of the building receive daylight through two grooves on either side of the lift shaft; at night they radiate reflected light thanks to the fact that the meter cupboards have been designed as ornamental lamps.

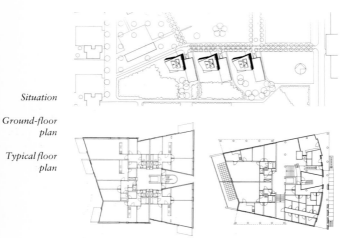

Situation

Ground-floor plan

Typical floor plan

Details:
closed façade,
open façade,
entrance,
meter cup-
board

From the report of the advisory committee for the 1993 Wibaut Prize (van Dijk *et al.*, 1993):

In the housing sector and in urban renewal in Amsterdam in recent years many projects have been realized where the designer adds an extra dimension to the town-planning layout given or interprets it in a surprising and enriching manner. Rudy Uytenhaak's three residential buildings on the Koningin Wilhelminaplein are exemplary proofs of this.

This building type – generally known as 'the urban villa' – often has a static and heavy character. That has been craftily avoided here by a lively interplay between curtain walls, screens placed on columns, and projecting eaves, which make the buildings reminiscent of large pavilions, completely apt in these surroundings. The façades of glass and red cedar placed at various angles cause a dynamism that is tempered by the orthogonally placed brick walls, which are closed apart from a few perforations. Not only does this give the separate buildings a charming, expressive effect, it also roots them in their surroundings. The conflict between the diverse directions of the surrounding buildings and the direction of the streets has been solved within the buildings themselves.

The spaces between the three blocks are both defined by a closed and an open façade, and the plant-covered roof of the half-sunken car-park. All the dwellings are oriented as much as possible towards the park's surroundings. In the exterior this is expressed in the balconies, where the need for shelter is also met by a closed balustrade. The way in which the building is entered, both by foot and car, is exemplary because of the openness and the generous dimensions of the entrances. (...)

The green surrounding the Slotervaart is a gift that not every housing architect is lucky enough to have. But the comprehensiveness and the talented way in which Uytenhaak has exploited the possibilities offered by these surroundings reveals an insight into town planning that few architects have. We therefore heartily recommend that the 1993 Wibaut Prize be awarded to Rudy Uytenhaak.

Urban plan and 104 dwellings, Coebel, Leiden
with: Marco Romano, Harry Pappot
commissioned by: Eurowoningen bv
designed: 1989

This project in Leiden reflects the experience gained in the design for the Koningin Wilhelminaplein, which showed that tunnel formwork does not necessarily lead to straitjacket architecture. By using the stairwell as a hinge for the rear tunnels, the effect of a fan-shaped flat is created. The ground floor and the top floor are also made using the same formwork.

This principle is used again in the plan for a residential tower on Insulindeweg in Amsterdam, a tower that is more dynamic and no longer a detached autonomous volume but half-fitted into an existing block, in a way similar to J.F. Staal's 'Wolkenkrabber' in Amsterdam (1930).

*Low-rise
housing*

78 dwellings, Vlaardingse Vaart, Vlaardingen
with: Ad van Aert, Jonathan Rose
commissioned by: Eurowoningen bv
designed: 1989
realized by: Aannemingsmaatschappij Panagro, 1992-93

The urban plan (by Ashok Bhalotra) prescribes a 'net curtain' of nine double villas and four tower blocks (sixteen dwellings on six floors) with a strong sculptural quality along the Vlaardingse Vaart. The dyke and the idea of transparency have led to a base with garage and bedrooms/workrooms with a living-room above in the form of a glass pavilion under a 'floating' roof. Originally, a more horizontal 'Villa Savoie' (Le Corbusier) was thought to be a suitable form here for the town-planning panacea offered by the 'urban villa'. Ultimately, programme requirements led to a prismatic tower of three dwellings per floor; the tower is hidden behind the cylindrically shaped balustrade, which acts as a veil.

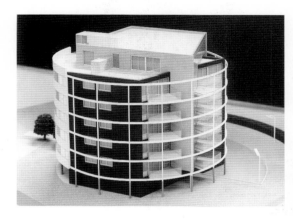

Tower, model

Ground-floor plan

Typical floor plan

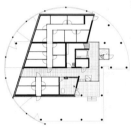

Model

52 dwellings, Thomas de Beer driehoek, Tilburg
with: Marco Romano
commissioned by: Bouwfonds Woningbouw bv
designed: 1992

The urban plan (by Mels Crouwel) proposes, in front of the entrance to the Museum De Pont, a 'modern court' in which there are four separate blocks. These apartment blocks were not to split up the court. Therefore an 'airy' abstract volume was sought for the (four times thirteen) dwellings.

The ground floor is largely kept free. The dwellings and terraces above are designed as a distinguished volume of dark-green stone. This 'Villa Savoie' layout produces an interplay between the simple oversized circumference and the complex volume it contains. Behind the larger openings in the circumference, light-reflecting 'silver' glass walls and balustrades ensure liveliness within the plain contour.

LOW-RISE/HIGH-DENSITY

It is not so much a question of mere density, but 'the quality of the density' or 'the density of qualities', a phenomenal density; figurative density instead of literal density. Urbanism arises from a density of functions, meanings and potentials.

From the relation between the qualities of a dwelling on the ground as such and the town-planning design, a degree of urbanism must be generated, where possible through an intensive fabric of dwellings and public spaces. Besides the specific aspects of the sites, specific forms of urban housing must be accentuated to reflect the heterogeneity of lifestyles and to obtain a differentiated and lively area in terms of function. Low-rise housing offers particular possibilities for this.

RUDY UYTENHAAK

Urban studies housing Geuzenveld, Amsterdam
with: Engbert van der Zaag, Theo Peppelman
commissioned by: Munic
designed: 1988

72 patio dwellings and 28 free-sector dwellings, Geuzenveld-West
with: Engbert van der Zaag
commissioned by: Stok & Proper, Rotterdam
designed: 1988
realized by: Hein Schilder, Volendam, 1991

Seventy-two dwellings enclosed in a neighbourhood of terraced houses acquired an introvert character by means of narrow streets, unusually intimate for a suburb. There are three types of dwelling; bungalow, family and housing for the elderly. The cars are parked in a carport behind the continuous wall surfaces, between streets and shared patios. This project can be seen as an exercise in 'mat' building.

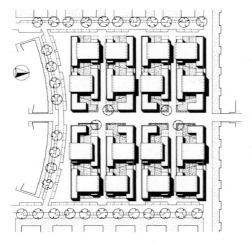

Situation

Ground-floor plan

First-floor plan

Urban study for low-rise high-density housing, north-east
quadrant, urban plan housing, north-west 3 quadrant, Nieuw
Sloten, Amsterdam
commissioned by: Dienst Volkshuisvesting
designed: 1988-89

399 dwellings, north-west quadrant, Nieuw Sloten
with: Engbert van der Zaag, Hugo Boogaard, Willem Grift
commissioned by: Dienst Volkshuisvesting, Nevanco
Woningbouw bv, bpf-bouw
designed: 1989-90
realized by: Nevanco Woningbouw bv, Bouwbedrijf
H. de Vries bv, 1992

The preliminary study 'Sleutels voor Sloten Noord-Oost' (Keys to
Sloten North-East) looked at the possibilities of a low-rise neighbourhood built up from terraced housing in a higher than normal density
(around seventy dwellings per hectare). The profiles of the urban plan
were developed as characteristically as possible, with, for example,
autonomous canal houses as a special double duplex and 'long houses'

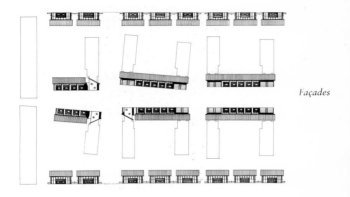

Façades

for the middle area. The plan eventually realized for 399 dwellings in Sloten North-West continues previous the study.

The design aims at a clearly differentiated and green spatial image, and to this end it accentuates the various town-planning profiles. The edges along the green waterside and park (built only five metres high) consist of very short rows, producing many end dwellings with a side entrance and a living-room on the street. Two different, long walls of narrow dwellings form the central urban space as the 'interior' of the neighbourhood. This space is filled in to produce an urban network of narrow streets, strongly related to one other and lined with broad and more introvert dwellings. One of the eight middle blocks is built as a courtyard (a reference to Pompeii). A symmetrical 'complex' is avoided by means of the asymmetric units stamped across the site, ensuring rhythmical series are created that lend diversity and cohesion to the neighbourhood. The result is more open than cluttered.

The goal of the architecture is to make concrete, in terms of function, size and material, and to reinforce the town-planning points of departure chosen: the garden city, green space, relaxed density, and sequences of different scales. It is an architecture of planes, large roof eaves, and a mildly abstract vernacular. Oblique bricks lend more relief to the walls.

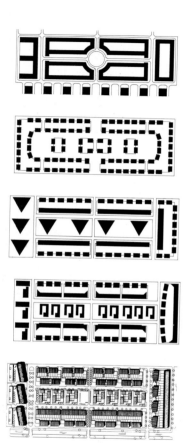

Stages in the design process, and final plan

Waterside, park edge and contrast in height

Relief in brickwork

Model

Urban plan Java-eiland, Amsterdam
with: Jan Peter Wingender, Mariëtte Adriaanssen, Ad van Aert,
Maurits Cobben
commissioned by: Projectgroep Oostelijk Havengebied
designed: 1991

This preliminary study for an urban plan considers the potential for achieving a ninety-nine per cent housing function while retaining a differentiated urban 'interior' for the island. The solution proposes 100 dwellings per hectare next to the inner city, yet in the wide open spaces of the waterscape.

Because dwellings on the ground can best generate vital urban space, the study emphasizes low-rise housing. In town-planning terms it argues in favour of approaching landscape, town-planning spaces and architecture as autonomous in scale and thus full of contrast, as 'situation', 'character' and 'meaningful detail'. By having the cross-section of the buildings slowly change, the urban spaces transform themselves to reflect the scale of the island.

Site plan

Urban study, Sporenburg, Amsterdam
with: Marco Romano, Joanne de Jager
commissioned by: Munic, New Deal
designed: 1993

The study for the Sporenburg 'Schierstad' ('peninsula city') is a continuation of the Java-eiland study. Maximizing the housing density (at 100
dwellings per hectare), with each house having its own front door and
private garage on the street, produces less public space with more potential. In this project a certain formality of the public space is aimed at,
with both a residential identity and an urban character.

The plan is based on seven different dwelling types and four types of
street (different in terms of profile, situation and appearance): these are
the ingredients for a 'minimal' town. Proceeding in the continuation of
the town, the space transforms itself as in a drawing by Escher or as in a
novel or film, the scenography gradually shifting under the changing cir-
cumstances.

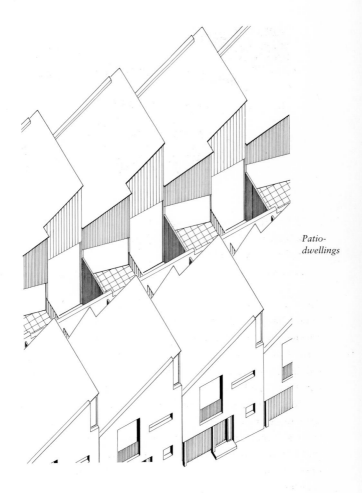

*Patio-
dwellings*

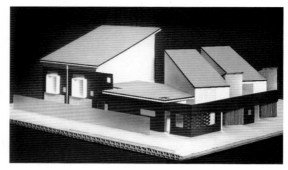

*Model,
corner study*

95 dwellings, Zaaneiland, Zaandam
with: Engbert van der Zaag
commissioned by: Bouwfonds
designed: 1992
realized by: Bouwbedrijf M.J. de Nijs & Zn bv, due 1994

'Village-like urban' buildings on an island in the river Zaan. Playing with individualities, volumes and views, they explore the density of elements within the accolade of a wall.

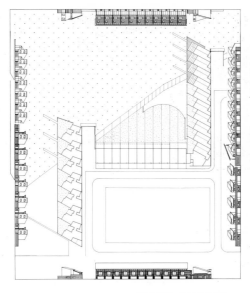

*Fragment of
urban plan
and façades*

Model

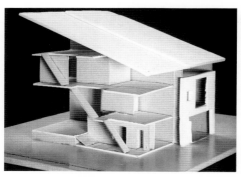

24 dwellings, Villabos, Amersfoort
with: Gé van Dam, Jonathan Rose
commissioned by: Bouwbedrijf Hoffmann bv
designed: 1989
realized by: Bouwbedrijf Hoffmann bv, 1993

'Villabos': slim limestone towers with white steel corners placed between the trees in response to the proposed town-planning theme of the 'wood of villas'.

ALTERATIONS AND CONVERSIONS

Although every design is a conversion, and can be seen as a confrontation between situation and design, in converting a building this confrontation is direct. Every intervention defines the interpretation of the existing building. New/old, what has priority at which point? How do you read the building, what are the rules that define the forms, do you aim at contrast or be subservient, do you reinforce what already exists? How do you investigate the existing qualities of the building on the basis of the proposed programme? How does the physical presence of the building affect you? Can you interweave new spaces? How do you keep the building's history legible? In layers?

RUDY UYTENHAAK

Apartment on Keizersgracht

Alterations to private houses, Keizersgracht, Binnen Dommersstraat, Prinsengracht, Amsterdam
commissioned by: Bierhaus and Uytenhaak, Martin family, Marjan van Essen
designed: 1975-79
realized by: Centraal Bouwbedrijf and others, 1975-80

Three exercises in unforced spatiality. The freedom of expression claimed, 'everything is permissible, if there is a motivation for it', leads to a divergence of resources. There is a complexity and dynamism in scale and form, as long as this benefits 'The Light'. In the margins of this the first discoveries in craftsmanship are made. And with this, while still at a very early stage, the capacity and the need not to desire everything.

The architect's own apartment in an Amsterdam canal house (Keizersgracht), a waterfall of stairs. A jeweller's studio with terrace, behind the top of a gable (Binnen Dommersstraat). A wood-frame dwelling in a shell (Prinsengracht), riddled with turning and falling light, routes and peepholes.

Apartment on Prinsengracht, floor plans and interior

*Jewellers'
studio,
Binnen
Dommers-
straat*

*Inner court,
façade*

60 dwellings, alterations to former fire station,
Nieuwe Achtergracht, Amsterdam
with: Ria Smit, Onno Vlaanderen
commissioned by: Onze Woning
designed: 1982-83
realized by: Koot's Bouwbedrijf, 1985

Meeting of two patterns. The old building (1907), solid and monumental, is used as a mantle for a new building. This new building is defined by the logic of social housing: it is compact, light and with repeating elements.

The two orders continually meet one another; the size and impact of the old generally prevails by making the new forms independent and abstract, with some accent provided by details or a touch of colour. It is the scale of the existing building that defines the character of the semi-public spaces: the courtyard, terraces, gallery and the monumental stairs. It respires the density of the dwellings. The dwellings, in turn, make the solid building more spacious and light. It is only in the centre that the new contents of the old building are fully revealed.

Entrance

Ground-floor plan

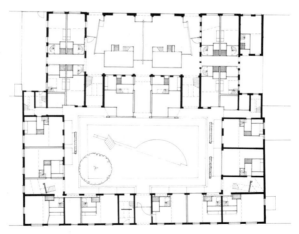

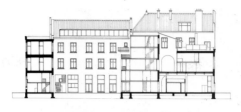

Cross-section

Gallery

Façade, detail

Conversion of a school into housing, Lepelkruisstraat, Amsterdam
with: Felix Claus, Ria Smit
commissioned by: Stichting Lieven de Key
designed: 1985
realized by: Bouwbedrijf Van Schaik bv, 1986

An old school building, originally horizontally organized, has been converted into three vertically accessed group dwellings. The rear façade, formerly enclosed, is now free and opened.

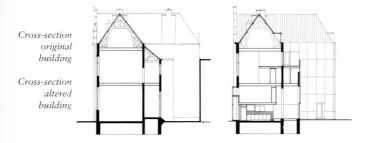

*Cross-section
original
building*

*Cross-section
altered
building*

Detail

Photographer's studio, Hempoint, Amsterdam
with: Felix Claus
commissioned by: C. Hutter
designed: 1986
realized by: Bouwbedrijf Van Schaik bv, 1986

Stairs, in their most primary legible form (uprights, steps and banisters),
link the various floors and ambiences in the foyer of a photographer's
studio.

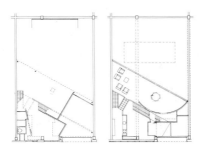

Floor plans

Roof pavilion

Apartment and roof pavilion, Amstel, Amsterdam
with: Harry Pappot
commissioned by: T. Strengers
designed: 1987
realized by: Bouwbedrijf E.A. van den Hengel bv, 1989

Light and material, the space of a penthouse. A history renewed below and on the roof of a monumental building, designed by Adriaan Dortsman (1625-82).

Apartment

*Exterior and
floor plans*

Interior

Alterations to an office building, Emmaplein, Amsterdam
with: Gerard Kruunenberg
commissioned by: Strating promotions
designed: 1987
realized by: Metalux, 1987

Eleven work areas in a single space, woven into an existing structure.

*Technical
details*

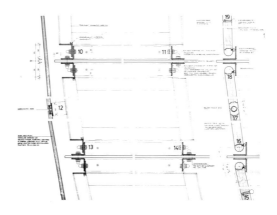

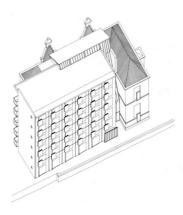

Guesthouse building, Plantage Muidergracht, Amsterdam
with: Hugo Boogaard, Kees Stoffels
commissioned by: Woonstichting De Doelen
designed: 1991
realized by: BV Aannemingsbedrijf J. Scheurer & Zn, 1993

The monumental spaces of an existing nineteenth-century school are now used as the portal to a new small *unité* of guest rooms for the University of Amsterdam.

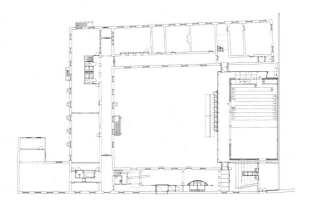

Centre for Art Education, Roermond
with: Engbert van der Zaag, Paul van der Erve
commissioned by: Municipality of Roermond
designed: 1991-93
realized by: Bruns & Bonke Aannemingsmaatschappij, due 1994

The inner courtyard of an old Jesuit monastery is closed by a music hall;
a solid hall contained within a glass hall. A box in a box.

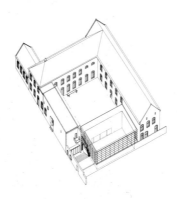

PARTICULAR PROJECTS

Even more than in the realization of more general quality, in certain particular programmes there is a desire to realize the individual values linked to those programmes. Here the essence of the programme is usually directly connected to the nature and form of its housing. These values are defined through direct contact with the client. Thus the architect's role becomes one of exploring the motives that are operating, revealing the possibilities and choices related to these, and then making the motives acquired and reformulated in this way the engine of the plan and the building process, which means the architect is devoted to the specific within general culture.

RUDY UYTENHAAK

Interior

Private house and studio, Zwolle
with: M.J. Rieder, Ria Smit
commissioned by: Rieder-Van den Eshof family
designed: 1982-84 and 1992-93
realized by: M.J. Rieder, 1985, and Majari, due 1994

This house for a furniture maker/contractor places a pronounced, yet nuanced, architecture in an old inner-city. It is spatial and material: light and 'modern', but at the same time strongly contextual.

The four outer walls are independent in form. In the somewhat detached façade the depth of the wall is built up in layers, which can be seen in the fifteen-centimetre-deep relief in the openings. This layered façade thus reflects the layered construction of the house. Inside the house the space develops in the depth of the volume, between the coulisses of the structural surfaces and diagonally upwards across the stairs. The interior, with the space-defining planes separated from one another and diverging lines creating a void 'escalating' to the corner, works as a mobile of light.

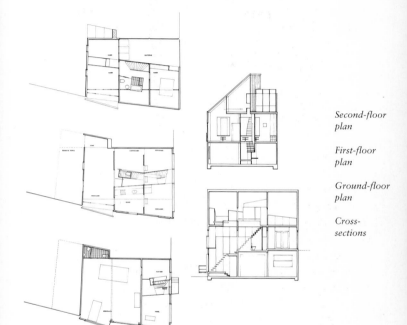

Second-floor plan

First-floor plan

Ground-floor plan

Cross-sections

Façade details

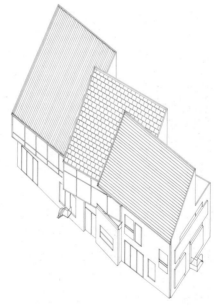

Extension,
due 1994

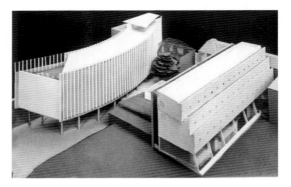

Model

Cultural Centre and offices, Grote Markt, Apeldoorn
competition entry, first prize
with: John Bosch, Gerard Kruunenberg
commissioned by: Munic
designed: 1988
not realized

A cultural centre and offices, with two existing buildings converted into
entrances, condense an inner-city 'block' and add a new layer of history.

Cross-sections

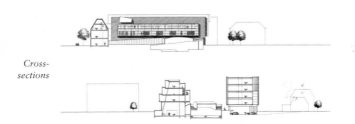

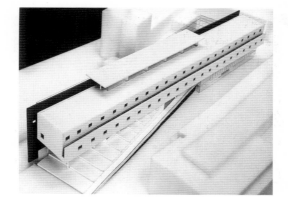

Model

Cultural Centre, Nieuwstraat, Apeldoorn
with: Arie van Harten, Gé van Dam, Tiemen Koetsier,
Jérôme Adema
commissioned by: Municipality of Apeldoorn
designed: 1990
realized by: Koopmans bv, Aannemingsbedrijf Ribberink bv, 1993

The cultural centre consists of a 'theatre' and an educational centre. Each has its own entrance and orientation. Inside there is a dense spatial interweaving of the identities that make up the complex, with a large wall acting as a guide.

In the heart of the building there is a junction between 'theatre' function below and 'school' function above. From here a ramp leads along the amphitheatre to a foyer and from there another, more spacious, ramp runs to the public entrances to the theatre. These entrances are flanked by a theatre café and the art-lending library, which is conceived as one large shop window on the inner-city side of the building. Under the gradually sloping roof of the building there are exhibition terraces, which rise like paddy-fields.

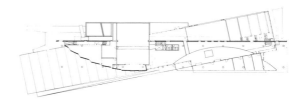

First-floor plan

Ground-floor plan

Basement

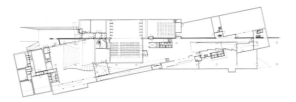

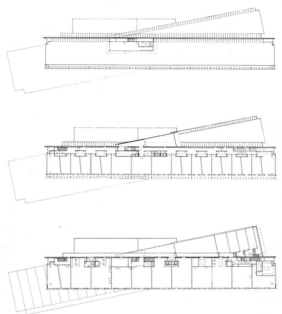

Fourth-floor plan

Third-floor plan

Second-floor plan

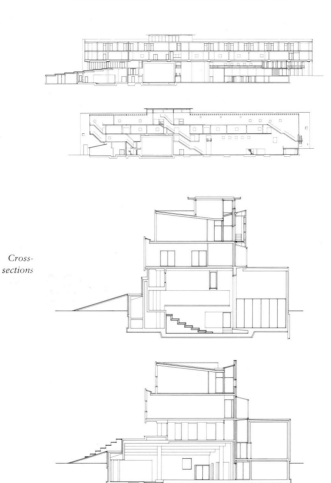

Cross-sections

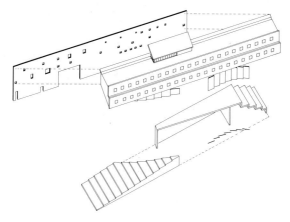

Exploded view

Model

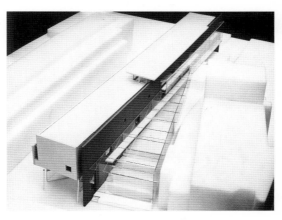

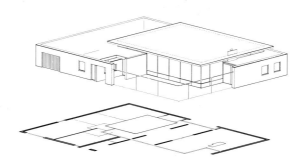

Villa, Amersfoort
with: Joost Hovenier
commissioned by: Zandstra family
designed: 1990
realized by: Lamoré bv, 1992

A villa made as an open pavilion surrounded and hidden by a wall of specially made stones, robuster in scale and visually richer than normal bricks.

Residential building, model

Office and dwellings, Juliana van Stolberglaan, Grotiusplaats,
The Hague
with: Engbert van der Zaag
commissioned by: Multivastgoed, Rijksgebouwendienst
designed: 1992

Two blocks, part of a crescendo of buildings. An exploration of scale
and skyline, the use of screens, light reflection and noise reduction.

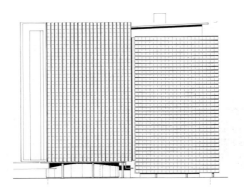

Office building

Model

Urban plan centre of Potsdam, Germany
with: Engbert van der Zaag, Tiemen Koetsier, Marco Romano,
Jan Peter Wingender
commissioned by: Municipality of Potsdam
designed: 1991

Potsdam, city with a damaged past. Intriguing case study illustrating the problem of the 'reconstruction of the European city'.

It is the topological structure that is of vital importance. Allow the special landscape quality of the valley of the river Havel to inspire a sort of urban therapy, with the lost and now 'empty' city centre being rediscovered. The old city, the 'water city', remaining for the time being principally a green bank open to the public, with a new stone water city on the southern side along the canal – the other city district, where the castle was formerly located, becoming the Capitol and Cultural Forum.

The main theme of the plan is the definition of four urban areas around the Havel, accompanying the development of an arcadian river valley. The infrastructure therefore needs to be related to the river on a new scale. Instead of the heavy cumbersome traffic bridge that denies the spatiality of city and landscape, there are four narrow transparent

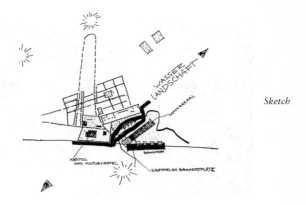

Sketch

bridges. The railway station, which forms a new bridgehead, is interpreted as the engine of the city, a transit harbour between various sorts
of traffic, and it acts as a link on three levels in the city: above, there is the
city terrace, on the quay a station square with a pedestrian bridge to the
old marketplace, and, half-way, a fragile tram viaduct. For motor traffic
there is a new bridge leading to the historically charged square of the old
castle. There, a special point marks the beginning of a series of large lin-
ear spaces (as is the case too in the main axis of the castle of Sansoucci).
A wire figure here in the centre of the Capitol represents the 'open hand'
(Le Corbusier) – a symbol of a new tolerant age? The fourth bridge is a
railway bridge, extremely significant for the new region.

*New wing,
under
construction*

Alterations and extension to town hall, Landsmeer
with: Ad van Aert, Engbert van der Zaag, Kees Stoffels
commissioned by: Municipality of Landsmeer
designed: 1991-92
realized by: Heddes Bouw bv, 1993

The current town hall of Landsmeer is neutrally modern and 'floating',
but therefore also somewhat detached and distant. The new entrance to
the administrative and public section in the existing building is therefore
built with some feeling for the ceremonial: the high awning above the
new entrance hall links the square to the wings, which are at right angles
to one another. Half outside, half inside, they also form an arcade on the
square with, on it, the 'shops' so to speak: the reception and interview
rooms.

The functional and constructional plan of the new building is efficient and economical. The interior is a complex interplay of different
layers (square, awning, arcade, rooms, offices and garden), divided by
more or less transparent screens.

*Model with
square*

Situation

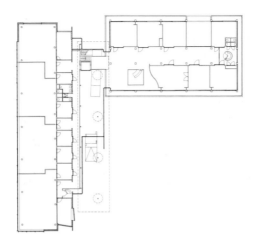

*First-floor
plan*

*Ground-floor
plan*

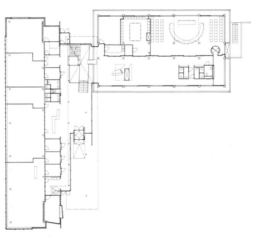

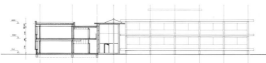

Interior new wing, under construction

Cross-section

New entrance

Arcade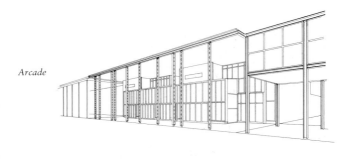

Shops and dwellings, Zeewolde
with: Joost Hovenier, Jan Peter Wingender
commissioned by: Projectbureau de Kant, B V Zeevoorde
designed: 1992
realized by: Burggraaff Bouw bv, 1993

Two patio dwellings and shopping space provide an arcade between the city library and a supermarket. The layered façade is an instrument to house a programme which is yet to be completely determined.

Arcade, under construction

Tiled façade

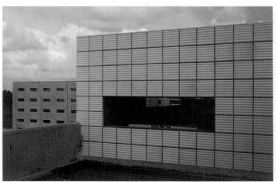

Chair

Stool

Chair, stool and cupboard
designed: 1972-77
realized: 1977

Cardboard chairs
with: Jérôme Adema
commissioned by: Munic
designed: 1993
realized by: Smurfit Loona Verpakking, 1993

Two chairs in multiplex and a series in cardboard, a cupboard of glass
and wood: exercises in material.

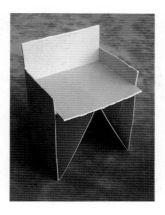

Cardboard chair

Cupboard

Cardboard theatre, Apeldoorn
with: Jérôme Adema
commissioned by: Munic
designed: 1993
realized by: Smurfit Loona Verpakking, 1993

A roof of cardboard wings, or are they tiles? For a temporary open-air theatre in and along the Apeldoorn Kanaal, to celebrate 'Apeldoorn 1200'.

BALANCE BETWEEN IDENTITY
AND COMPOSITION

What gives an architectural *œuvre* its force? Is it the theory, the conceptual side, which distinguishes the architect's work from just the average building production? Is it a personal signature, or is it rather the sublime adaptation of a classical style?

As an arrangement of place and function, architecture has a clear social significance. In the twentieth century architects have laid much emphasis on this side of their work. Both the rise of the socialist-oriented modern movement in the 1920s and the humanist reaction to international modernism in the 1960s can be seen as a reaction by architects to the state in which their profession then found itself, seen from a social perspective.

Does this engagement still have any importance in the development of a high-quality architecture, or can the architect today do nothing else but express the primacy of the autonomy of his artistry in the exercise of his profession? No absolute answer can be given to this sort of question, but it does outline the problems on which an architect must take a position with his work.

The work of Rudy Uytenhaak is not known for out-spoken architectural-theoretical stances, nor for a strong emphasis on the conceptual side of architecture. His projects have a characteristic expression in which knowledge of the rules of twentieth-century modern architectural aesthetics, in particular, can be recognized. Without being a formalist, he gives his work a post-modern character by reinterpreting these sources of inspiration. But the personal way in which inspirations are incorporated, supported by an unorthodox use of colour and material, rich in contrasts, save it from the risk of being fashionable.

A purely stylistic consideration of this architecture would be too limited to touch on its essence. What is most characteristic in Uytenhaak's work are the themes in the design that are related to the demarcating and connecting of spaces and functions, not only as a purely compositional theme but also as a means of giving spaces identity in relation to their use. From his first well-known work, the conversion of a former fire station into sixty dwellings on Nieuwe Achtergracht in Amsterdam (1985), the expression of and ascription of meaning to the boundaries of spaces has played a leading role in his architecture. In this case Uytenhaak appreciated the characteristic architecture of the existing building and used it to convey the new identity of this housing complex. Within the structure of the building, he designed a new layout of private-housing areas with balconies, loggias and terraces, sheltered entrances in a communal interior, an inner courtyard as the core of the complex, and some new entrances in the original exterior porches. He arranged the new uses within the existing building in such a way that its structure and contents remained clearly recognizable. The main layout is defined by the original structure; the contents are emphasized by infills, like screens, placed behind or in front of the original walls. In this way the character of the existing building is used to define the communal identity of the new housing complex as a whole, while, by using contrasting material, colour and composition, the various infills work towards a recognition of the identity of individual residents, without overshadowing the communal interior of the complex.

Landsmeer town hall · The extension to the town hall in Landsmeer (1993) is an exercise in the aesthetics of separating and linking, applied to the visualization of a significant spot in a village community. Beside the original town hall by M.F. Duintjer, an uninspired 1960s building in the International Style with horizontal strips of windows and concrete eaves on each floor set back from the village building line, Uytenhaak designed an office wing at a right angle to the building line. Although it deviates sharply in architectural terms, the end of this wing fits into the scale of the buildings and heralds the town-hall square bordered on two sides by the new wing and the existing building. Seen from the square the new building reveals itself as a series of entirely or partially transparent screens, slid next to each other. Above this a horizontal slab floats as a canopy under which the monumental public entrance, hall and ceremonial staircase are located.

Next to this entrance zone the two-storey building has on both floors a corridor and a strip containing service spaces and meeting rooms. Between the corridors and the strip there is a screen of regularly positioned white posts, which protrudes beyond the building volume at both ends to accentuate the division between the public section and the administrative offices, the latter being housed in a longitudinal block with floors that can be laid out freely. The new layout of the existing town hall, too, is the visualization of the theme of zoning and screening. As a result, the building as a whole can be seen as a filter between the public, which uses in both wings the sides facing the square, and the officials and the administration, who are housed at the rear sides of the existing building and the new wing respectively.

Czaar Peterbuurt · Uytenhaak's many years of involvement with the urban renewal of Amsterdam's Czaar Peterbuurt acquired concrete shape in two realized projects. They can be seen as a response to the existing morphology of narrow closed blocks and long straight streets.

The 'housing *palazzi*' on Conradstraat (1990) are composed of strips of dwellings which are placed in pairs mirroring each other; each pair is treated as a formal unit which, in turn, is part of a series of four identical buildings. All four have a tight, closed character on the exterior, in which the individual dwelling is not emphasized. On this exterior a palace typology is used, with a cornice formed by the roof overhang and the strip window of the top storey, a projecting central section of the balconies of the middle dwellings, located in a regular and symmetrical façade, and a basement accentuated somewhat by a semi-colonnade. In the end walls the cut-off roof eaves and the horizontal bands of the pergolas that border the entrance court accentuate the compositional unity of the pairs of strips.

On the other hand, on the side of the communal

*Town hall
Landsmeer,
new wing*

entrance court each dwelling is identifiable. Although this entrance court is completely open on both sides, the character of an inner courtyard is evoked by the pergolas and because the walls are designed here to be much freer and lighter, like transparent screens with balconies. The glass fronts of the corner dwellings are placed at an angle, so that these dwellings are oriented to the exterior and the entrance court is also more sheltered.

The adjacent buildings between Conradstraat and Czaar Peterstraat show, within the neutrality of a site typology of closed blocks, that it is possible to give the impression of various types of dwellings in the street wall. The project also shows how a cramped block can be opened up without disturbing the existing urban structure. The Conradstraat façade is constructed from four identical blocks of apartments four floors high, a building form reminiscent of the *palazzine*, apartment blocks built very close together in certain neighbourhoods in Rome in the 1950s and '60s.

Right behind these blocks is the long six-storey-high building in Czaar Peterstraat. The lower two floors of this building offer space for maisonettes with gardens, as well as commercial premises and entrances and storage spaces for the upper dwellings. The next three floors contain two-bedroom apartments, which are reached from above or below by a gallery at the rear of the third floor. The top floor consists of two-bedroom apartments with a gallery at the back. All the dwellings have their living-room and sun-facing balcony on Czaar Peterstraat and, as much as possible, their bedrooms and kitchen with a smaller balcony at the back. The maisonettes, commercial premises and entrance portals in the lower part of the building each have their own individual façades over two

*Czaar
Peterbuurt,
housing*

floors, which together form one double-storey plinth. The middle section of the three floors above this has a regular pattern of identical windows, supplemented on the middle floor by a balcony with a balustrade of perforated steel in which a figure is depicted for each dwelling; the figures are based on a design by Ruudt Peeters and serve to distinguish, albeit minimally, each dwelling within the block as a whole. The top floor is accentuated by recessing the glass-fronted façade to create the effect of attics, and by having the balcony strip with transparent balustrade hang over rather like a cornice.

The street wall is thus given an extremely regular, classical composition, one which also has a clear beginning and end in the form of differently realized end walls. The character of the façades as screens is emphasized by the vertical openings used in the end walls. Uytenhaak's fascination with the partial screening off and partial connecting of spaces is also significant in morphological terms. The gradual opening of the structure of closed blocks to the detached *palazzi* via *palazzine* means that even the dwellings on Czaar Peterstraat have a view, however restricted, of the water of the Oosterburgervaart. The public space is thus differentiated from street and garden into court, green and quay.

Nieuw Sloten · In the plan for Nieuw Sloten the theme of communality and individuality is translated to the scale of a composition for a residential district as a whole. In the town-planning scheme a clear structure has been given to the public space, in which a hierarchy of park, waterside greenery, avenue, street and residential path guarantees a good orientation; this spatial hierarchy does not reflect a social hierarchy however. The blocks are designed as part of a composition for the site as a whole, but they are also conceived as a compositional unity in themselves. Each block is rooted in the public space by adding nuances to the entrance areas specific to each spot. The identity of the individual dwelling is achieved by emphasizing the entrance areas of each dwelling separately in the linked building, while in the multi-storey building the entrance area of each block and the balconies or loggias of each dwelling are emphasized. With all types of linked or stacked dwellings Uytenhaak uses a screen of masonry on the street side. In most cases a volume of glass walls and light façade cladding protrudes above this, capped with generous roof overhangs. Where the screen of the façade continues over a number of floors, it is assembled from a semi-colonnade with, below, various glass walls that serve as an entrance, in the middle a regular pattern of windows, and above, in the façade walls, a series of occasional *oculi*. A block is always reduced to countable units. With special corner solutions, incidental additions in front, changing dwelling types and various nuances in colour and details of masonry, glass and wall cladding, Uytenhaak differentiates the composition of the blocks in each area within the neighbourhood. This led to the creation of an extremely varied residential neighbourhood – within the outlines of a clearly formulated site scheme in which each of the dwellings has a meaningful place within the whole.

Polarity · The theme of the balance between the composition as a whole and the identity of each part within it, or, to put it another way, the balance between the communal and the individual, is a leitmotiv in Uytenhaak's *œuvre*. It can be deduced from this that it is possible to both regard this basic theme as purely compositional and also to understand it as a response to the role of the architect in society. The ideas recognizable in his work are derived from both classical and early modern architectural principles, and from architectural realizations of humanist theories in the Netherlands propounded by the *Forum* generation (Aldo van Eyck and others). Uytenhaak further develops these ideas and principles within the contemporary tasks of architecture and urban design. He does not cherish the ideological content of either the modern movement or the humanist reaction to the International Style; instead he tests it to see whether it is valid for our times.

Uytenhaak's work shows that the heritage of both the pioneers of modern Dutch architecture (the so-called Nieuwe Bouwen) and *Forum* can be more significant for the tasks of contemporary architecture than detached salon critiques with slogan titles like 'Modernism without dogma' or rhetorical manipulations like 'How modern is Dutch Architecture?' would lead us to believe. In his projects, the relationship between the eclectic modern content and the humanist content is extremely different (see, for example, the building on Weesperstraat or the neighbourhood of Nieuw Sloten). It is this polarity that Uytenhaak wants to suggest is an issue of importance for contemporary architecture. Thus he has not withdrawn into the autonomy of architecture in reaction to the hardening and individualization of society in the 1980s and '90s; he has actually sought to express in a balanced manner the identity of the individual within an architectural composition.

JORIS MOLENAAR

Nieuw Sloten

1949	Born in Amsterdam, 17 April
1967-73	Studied architecture at the Technische Hogeschool in Eindhoven
1972-80	Worked at various bureaus, including Girod & Groeneveld, Van Eyck & Bosch
1973-75	Academic staff member at the Technische Hogeschool in Eindhoven
1975-	Teacher at the Academie van Bouwkunst in Amsterdam
1978-84	Editor of *Forum*
1979-82	Member of governing body of Architectura et Amicitia
1980-	Independent practice in Amsterdam
1980-84	Visiting lecturer at the Technische Universiteit in Delft
1985-88	Group exhibitions in Amsterdam, Antwerp, Zurich, Eindhoven and Delft
1987-	Visiting lecturer in Toronto, Karslruhe, Leuven, Munich
1990-93	Professor architectural and town-planning design at the Technische Universiteit in Eindhoven
1991	Beton Prize for Droogbak housing
1993	Wibaut Prize for Koningin Wilhelminaplein housing

Chair
  designed: 1972-77, *realized:* 1977;
Urban plan for Vrijthof, Maastricht
  competition entry, in co-operation with A. v.d. Eerenbeemt,
  designed: 1972, *not realized*;
Alterations to a private house, Keizersgracht, Amsterdam
  commissioned by: Bierhaus and Uytenhaak, *designed:* 1975,
  realized: 1976;
Alterations to a private house, Binnen Dommersstraat, Amsterdam
  commissioned by: Martin family, *designed:* 1975-79, *realized:*
  1975-80;
Stool
  designed: 1977, *realized:* 1977;
Cupboard
  designed: 1977, *realized:* 1977;
Alterations to a private house, Prinsengracht, Amsterdam
  commissioned by: Marjan van Essen, *designed:* 1977, *realized by:*
  Centraal Bouwbedrijf, 1978;
Schinkel house
  competition entry, *designed:* 1979, *not realized*;
Garden house, Amsterdam
  commissioned by: Hannie Rentjes, *designed:* 1980, *realized:* 1982;
First urban plan Weesperstraat, Amsterdam
  commissioned by: Buurtcomité Weesperbuurt, *designed:* 1980;
Shops and housing, Lindengracht, Amsterdam
  commissioned by: D. Kars, *designed:* 1981, *not realized*;
Urban plan Czaar Peterbuurt, Amsterdam
  commissioned by: Comité Behoud en Herstel, *designed:* 1980-81;
Alterations to 3 apartments, Keizersgracht, Amsterdam
  commissioned by: Owners' Association Keizersgracht 682,
  Verhulst family and C. Brinkgreve, *designed:* 1982/87,
  realized by: 1982/87;

Urban plan Oostenburg Zuid, Amsterdam
commissioned by: Comité Behoud en Herstel, *designed:* 1982;
Private house and studio, Zwolle
commissioned by: Rieder-Van den Eshof family, *designed:* 1982-
84, *realized by:* M.J. Rieder, 1985;
60 dwellings, alterations to former fire station, Nieuwe Achtergracht,
Amsterdam
commissioned by: Onze Woning, *designed:* 1982-83, *realized by:*
Koot's Bouwbedrijf, 1985;
Urban plan Rijkskledingmagazijnen, Conradstraat, Amsterdam
commissioned by: Projectgroep Oostelijke eilanden and Comité
Behoud en Herstel, *designed:* 1984;
Alterations to a private house, Keizersgracht 74, Amsterdam
commissioned by: T. Uytenhaak, *designed:* 1984, *realized:* 1985;
Conversion of a school into housing, Lepelkruisstraat, Amsterdam
commissioned by: Stichting Lieven de Key, *designed:* 1985, *realized
by:* Bouwbedrijf Van Schaik bv, 1986;
Alterations to 10 dwellings, 2e Oosterparkstraat, Amsterdam
commissioned by: Stichting Lieven de Key, *designed:* 1985-87,
realized by: Bouwbedrijf Van Schaik bv, 1987;
Alterations to a private house, Van Eegenstraat, Amsterdam
commissioned by: Bierhaus and Uytenhaak, *designed:* 1985,
realized: 1985;
Dentist's practice, Nicolaas Maesstraat, Amsterdam
commissioned by: B. Molendijk, *designed:* 1986, *realized:* 1986;
Photographer's studio, Hempoint, Amsterdam
commissioned by: C. Hutter, *designed:* 1986, *realized by:*
Bouwbedrijf Van Schaik bv, 1986;
95 dwellings and parking, Droogbak, Amsterdam
commissioned by: Stichting Lieven de Key, *designed:* 1986, *realized
by:* Smit's Bouwbedrijf, 1989;

141 dwellings, Conradstraat, Amsterdam
  commissioned by: Woningbouwvereniging Eigen Haard, *designed:*
  1985-86, *realized by:* Grootel's Bouwmaatschappij bv, 1990;
Second urban plan Weesperstraat, Amsterdam
  in co-operation with residents, municipality and others,
  commissioned by: Munic, *designed:* 1986;
56 dwellings and parking, Lepelstraat/Weesperstraat, Amsterdam
  commissioned by: Onze Woning, *designed:* 1986-87, *not realized;*
Design for two office buildings, Weesperstraat, Amsterdam
  commissioned by: M.A.B., *designed:* 1986-87, *not realized;*
205 dwellings, 2 shops, 15 offices, lunchroom and parking,
Weesperstraat/Nieuwe Kerkstraat, Amsterdam
  commissioned by: Onze Woning, *designed:* 1986-88, *realized by:*
  Smit's Bouwbedrijf, 1992;
Alterations to an office building, Emmaplein, Amsterdam
  commissioned by: Strating promotions, *designed:* 1987, *realized by:*
  Metalux, 1987;
Alterations and extension to a garden house, Amstel, Amsterdam
  commissioned by: D. Saire, *designed:* 1987, *not realized;*
Apartment and roof pavilion, Amstel, Amsterdam
  commissioned by: T. Strengers, *designed:* 1987, *realized by:*
  Bouwbedrijf E.A. van den Hengel bv, 1989;
Alterations to a private house, Willemsparkweg, Amsterdam
  commissioned by: Rijksbaron family, *designed:* 1988, *realized:*
  1988;
Urban studies housing Geuzenveld, Amsterdam
  commissioned by: Munic, *designed:* 1988;
72 patio dwellings and 28 free-sector dwellings, Geuzenveld-West,
Amsterdam
  commissioned by: Stok & Proper, Rotterdam, *designed:* 1988,
  realized by: Hein Schilder, Volendam, 1991;

28 dwellings, Sumatraplantsoen/Tidorestraat, Amsterdam
commissioned by: Gemeentelijk Woningbedrijf and Huib Bakker,
designed: 1988, *realized by:* Huib Bakker, 1991;

Cultural Centre and offices, Grote Markt, Apeldoorn
competition entry, *commissioned by:* Munic, *designed:* 1988,
not realized;

Urban study for low-rise high-density housing, north-east quadrant,
Nieuw Sloten, Amsterdam
commissioned by: Dienst Volkshuisvesting, *designed:* 1988;

Urban plan Groothandelsmarktterrein, The Hague
commissioned by: Munic, *designed:* 1987-88;

123 dwellings and parking, Koningin Wilhelminaplein, Amsterdam
commissioned by: bpf-bouw, *designed:* 1989, *realized by:*
Bouwbedrijf Teerenstra bv, 1991;

Urban plan housing, north-west 3 quadrant, Nieuw Sloten, Amsterdam
commissioned by: Dienst Volkshuisvesting, *designed:* 1989;

297 dwellings, north-west quadrant, Nieuw Sloten, Amsterdam
commissioned by: Dienst Volkshuisvesting and Nevanco
Woningbouw bv, *designed:* 1989-90, *realized by:* Nevanco
Woningbouw bv, 1992;

102 dwellings, north-west quadrant, Nieuw Sloten, Amsterdam
commissioned by: bpf-bouw, *designed:* 1989, *realized by:*
Bouwbedrijf H. de Vries bv, 1992;

Study patio dwellings, Zoetermeer
commissioned by: Stok & Proper, *designed:* 1989;

Urban plan and 104 dwellings, Coebel, Leiden
commissioned by: Eurowoningen bv, *designed:* 1989;

40 dwellings and an office, Rijnsburgse Singel, Leiden
competition entry, *commissioned by:* Woningbouwvereniging Ons
Doel, *designed:* 1989, *not realized;*

Feasibility study, alterations to housing for elderly people, Groningen
 commissioned by: Stichting Groninger Woningbouw Concordia,
 designed: 1989;
78 dwellings, Vlaardingse Vaart, Vlaardingen
 commissioned by: Eurowoningen bv, *designed:* 1989, *realized by:*
Aannemingsmaatschappij Panagro, 1992-93;
24 dwellings, Villabos, Amersfoort
 commissioned by: Bouwbedrijf Hoffmann bv, *designed:* 1989,
 realized by: Bouwbedrijf Hoffmann bv, 1993;
Urban plan Hobbemastraat, The Hague
 in co-operation with s o g z, *commissioned by:* Municipality of
 The Hague, *designed:* 1990;
Housing and shops, Hobbemastraat, The Hague
 commissioned by: VZOS, municipality of The Hague, Stedelijk
 Belang, Dienst Parkeerbeheer, Woningbouwvereniging
 's Gravenhage, *designed:* 1990, *realized by:* Wilma Bouw bv, 1993;
Urban plan Maria ten Hoorn, Groningen
 commissioned by: Dienst Bouwen+Woningen, Groningen,
 designed: 1990;
Feasibility study, alterations to portico housing, Schilderswijk, The
Hague
 commissioned by: P.O.S. and Woningbouwvereniging
 's Gravenhage, *designed:* 1990;
Cultural Centre, Nieuwstraat, Apeldoorn
 commissioned by: Municipality of Apeldoorn, *designed:* 1990,
 realized by: Koopmans bv and Aannemingsbedrijf Ribberink bv,
 1993;
95 dwellings and 4 offices, Czaar Peterstraat, Amsterdam
 commissioned by: Woningbouwvereniging Eigen Haard, *designed:*
 1990, *realized by:* Grootel's Bouwmaatschappij bv 1993;

Villa, Amersfoort
commissioned by: Zandstra family, *designed:* 1990, *realized by:* Lamoré bv, 1992;

Urban plan centre of Potsdam, Germany
commissioned by: Municipality of Potsdam, *designed:* 1991;

Urban plan Java-eiland, Amsterdam
commissioned by: Projectgroep Oostelijk Havengebied, *designed:* 1991;

Urban plan local-authority district office, Buitenveldert, Amsterdam
commissioned by: Blauwhoed, *designed:* 1991;

Alterations to an office, Jan Luykenstraat, Amsterdam
commissioned by: R. Uytenhaak, *designed:* 1991, *realized by:* Bouwbedrijf Van Schaik bv, 1991;

Alterations and extension to town hall, Landsmeer
commissioned by: Municipality of Landsmeer, *designed:* 1991-92, *realized by:* Heddes Bouw bv, 1993;

Centre for Art Education, Roermond
commissioned by: Municipality of Roermond, *designed:* 1991-93, *realized by:* Bruns & Bonke Aannemingsmaatschappij, due 1994;

Alterations and new guesthouse building, Plantage Muidergracht, Amsterdam
commissioned by: Woonstichting De Doelen, *designed:* 1991, *realized by:* BV Aannemingsbedrijf J. Scheurer & Zn, 1993;

Urban study Czaar Peterbuurt, Amsterdam
commissioned by: Projectgroep Oostelijke eilanden and Munic, *designed:* 1992;

Office and dwellings, J. van Stolberglaan, Grotiusplaats, The Hague
commissioned by: Multivastgoed and Rijksgebouwendienst, *designed:* 1992;

Shops and dwellings, Zeewolde
commissioned by: Projectbureau de Kant and BV Zeevoorde, *designed:* 1992, *realized by:* Burggraaff Bouw bv, 1993;

52 dwellings, Thomas de Beer driehoek, Tilburg
commissioned by: Bouwfonds Woningbouw bv, *designed:* 1992;
Cardboard theatre and chairs, Apeldoorn
commissioned by: Munic, *designed:* 1993, *realized by:* Smurfit
Loona Verpakking, 1993;
95 dwellings, Zaaneiland, Zaandam
commissioned by: Bouwfonds, *designed:* 1992, *realized by:*
Bouwbedrijf M.J. de Nijs & Zn bv, due 1994;
10 dwellings Lijnbaansgracht, Amsterdam
commissioned by: De Jong bv, *designed:* 1992-93;
Urban study, Sporenburg, Amsterdam
commissioned by: Munic and New Deal, *designed:* 1993;
36 dwellings, Landsmeer
commissioned by: Nevanco Woningbouw bv, *designed:* 1993,
realized by: Nevanco Woningbouw bv, due 1994;
180 dwellings Java-eiland, Amsterdam
commissioned by: bpf-bouw, *designed:* 1993, *realized by:*
Bouwcombinatie Java-eiland, due 1994-;
Residential towers Javaplantsoen, Amsterdam
commissioned by: Bouwbedrijf Teerenstra bv, *designed:* 1993,
realized by: Bouwbedrijf Teerenstra bv, due 1994-;
27 dwellings, Czaar Peterbuurt, Amsterdam
commissioned by: Woningbouwver. Eigen Haard, *designed:* 1993;
Guesthouses, Plantage Muidergracht, Amsterdam
commissioned by: Woonstichting De Doelen, *designed:* 1993,
realized by: B V Aannemingsbedrijf J. Scheurer & Zn, due 1994;
Extension to the private house, Zwolle, realized in 1985
in co-operation with M.J. Rieder, *commissioned by:* Rieder family,
designed: 1992-93, *realized by:* Majari, due 1994.

'A Creative? Tradition? Bruno Taut, a creative? Tradition!', *Forum* (theme number) no. 6 1977.

'Collage city', *Forum* no. 1 1980, pp. 34-35.

'Klontjes', *Forum* no. 1 1980, pp. 5-7.

'Gebouw en stad', *Forum* no. 2 1980, p. 52.

'Het vrijer maken van vorm en associatie. Werk van Koen van Velsen', *Forum* no. 2 1980, p. 18.

'Gebouw zonder idee negeert de stad', *Futura* no. 7/8 1981, pp. 2-6.

'Stopera: geen idee van de stad', *Forum* no. 3 1981, pp. 18-19.

'Vormgeven aan een karakteristiek', *Forum* no. 4 1984, pp. 42-45.

Ruimte dichten. Opdracht, visie en passie [Inaugural lecture, 15 February 1991], Technische Universiteit Eindhoven.

Is architectuur boventallig? [Valedictory lecture, 5 February 1993], Technische Universiteit Eindhoven.

1983

Tulleners, Hans, 'Dakpaviljoen op Amsterdams pandje', *Eigen huis en interieur* no. 2 1983, pp. 50-53.

1985

A'85, exhibition catalogue, Stichting Wonen, 24 February-13 December 1985.

1986

Debets, Carla, 'Wonen in "de Brandweer": contrast tussen oud en nieuw', *Bouwwereld* no. 7 1986, pp. 14-17.

Kloos, Maarten, 'Een oudhollands hofje, stijl 1986', *De Volkskrant* 12 February 1986.

'Nieuwe Achtergracht 40-96, Voormalige Stadstimmertuinen 35-89', in: Gemeentelijke Dienst Volkshuisvesting Amsterdam (ed.), *Sociale Woningbouw Amsterdam '68-'86*, Amsterdam 1986, p. 47.

Rodermond, Janny, 'Verbouwing Amsterdamse brandweerkazerne. Contrastrijk weefsel van oud en nieuw', *De Architect* no. 3 1986, pp. 37-43.

1987

Gids voor moderne architectuur in Nederland, Rotterdam 1987, p. 50.

1988

Kloos, Maarten, 'Rudy Uytenhaak', *Architecture d'Aujourd'hui*, no. 257 1988, pp. 58-61.

Uytenhaak, Rudy, 'Woningen in voormalig schoolgebouw te Amsterdam', *Bouw* no. 7 1988, pp. 29-31.

1990

Bergen, Tanja van, 'Een kikkervisje tussen spoor en de Houttuinen', *Het Parool* 14 April 1990.

Confurius, Gerrit, 'Wohnungen in einer Feuerwache', *Bauwelt* no. 26 1990, pp. 1332-1337.

Confurius, Gerrit, 'Neues aus Amsterdam. De Nieuwe Droogbak', *Bauwelt* no. 31 1990, pp. 1528-1533.

Confurius, Gerrit, 'Mit Schief aufgesezter Mütze und Brille', *Bauwelt* no. 38 1990, pp. 1940-1941.

'De Eindhovense School', *Forum* no. 4 1990, pp. 18-19.

Köhne, J.H., 'Beton in Beeld. Wonen tussen verkeer en stad', *Cement* no. 6 1990, pp. 36-41.

'Markant gebouw als deel van de stad', in: Brouwers, Ruud (ed.), *Architecture in the Netherlands. Yearbook 1989-1990*, Deventer 1990, pp. 94-97.

Morteo, Enrico, 'Rudy Uytenhaak, Edificio residenziale "De Droogbak" Amsterdam', *Domus* no. 723 1990, pp. 50-59.

Oosterman, Arjen, 'Een gebouw voor de stad. Woningbouw van Rudy Uytenhaak in Amsterdam', *Archis* no. 3 1990, pp. 36-41.

Rebois, Didier, 'Le logement social aux Pays-Bas', *Le Moniteur Architecture* no. 16 1990, pp. 26-35.

Rodermond, Janny, 'Stijlvol in nuances. Woongebouw "de Droogbak" van Rudy Uytenhaak', *De Architect* no. 2 1990, pp. 30-37.

Stoutjesdijk, Hans, 'Palazzo's in de Csaar Peter buurt. Uytenhaak introduceert nieuw verkavelingstype', *De Architect* no. 9 1990, pp. 100-105.

Uytenhaak, Rudy, 'Huurwoningen in palazzo's. Rudy Uytenhaak transformeert Amsterdamse oostelijke eilanden', *Architectuur/ Bouwen* no. 10 1990, pp. 14-16.

Weston, Richard, 'Dutch Delight', *Architects' Journal* vol. 191 no. 24 1990, pp. 36-43.

'Woongebouw de Droogbak te Amsterdam', *Bouw* no. 14/15 1990, pp. 24-29.

1991

Eldonk, Jos van and Hans Stoutjesdijk, 'Amsterdam experimenteert
met nieuwe aanpak. Woningbouw in Geuzenveld-West',
De Architect no. 11 1991, pp. 110-111.

Kapitzki, Christel (ed.), *Auf der Suche nach dem verlorenen Bild*,
Potsdam 1991.

Maas, Tom, Hans Stoutjesdijk and Rudy Uytenhaak, 'Friede den
Palästen', *Bauwelt* no. 11 1991, pp. 488-493.

Molenaar, Joris, 'Een amalgaam van hoven en stroken. Conradstraat
Amsterdam', in: Brouwers, Ruud (ed.), *Architecture in the
Netherlands. Yearbook 1990-1991*, Rotterdam 1991, pp. 136-139.

Polito, Salvatore, 'Housing in Amsterdam', *L'Industria delle
construzione* no. 239 1991, p. 50-55.

Rebois, Didier, 'Logements Amsterdam', *Le Moniteur Architecture*
no. 26 1991, p. 22.

'Settlement in Droogbak', *Arkitektur B* no. 47/48 1991, pp. 144-147.

Uytenhaak, Rudy, 'Woonblock in Droogbak Amsterdam, 1990', *Werk,
Bauen + Wonen* no. 11 1991, pp. 48-53.

1992

'Coulisssen in het park. Kon. Wilhelminaplein Amsterdam', in:
Brouwers, Ruud (ed.), *Architecture in the Netherlands. Yearbook
1991-1992*, Rotterdam 1992, pp. 64-65.

'Dialoog met de genius loco. Tidorestraat e.o.', in: Brouwers, Ruud
(ed.), *Architecture in the Netherlands. Yearbook 1991-1992*,
Rotterdam 1992, pp. 66-67.

Haan, Hilde de and Ids Haagsma, 'Monument van goede bedoelingen
aan de Weesperstraat', *De Volkskrant* 31 December 1992.

Jong, Hanneke de, 'Een raadhuis met "zingende lijnen" kern in
Landsmeer', *Nieuwe Noordhollandse Courant* 6 June 1992.

Kaspori, Dennis *et al.* (eds), 'De Eindhovense School', exhibition catalogue, *De Omslag* no. 7½ 1992.

Koster, Egbert, 'De aaibaarheidsfactor van architectuur', *Architectuur en Bouwen* no. 9 1992, pp. 22-30.

Ravesteijn, Albert, 'Schilderswijk in Den Haag. Stadterneurung und Rekonstruktion', *Bauwelt* no. 31 1992, pp. 1742-1749.

Zweers, Arnold, 'Oude stad moet je zien als een soort humus waarop het nieuwe groeit', *Apeldoornse Courant* 10 June 1992.

1993

Dijk, Hans van, Rein Geurtsen and Lucien Lafour, *Rapport adviescommissie Wibautprijs 1993*, June 1993 (unpublished).

Gameren, Dick van, 'Terug naar het AUP. Woningbouw Koningin Wilhelminaplein Amsterdam', *De Architect* no. 1 1993, pp. 49-54.

Kuperus, Marga and Dienst Stadsontwikkeling Gemeente Amersfoort, *De Villa's van Zielhorst. Maatwerk in architectuur*, Amersfoort 1993.

Rodermond, Janny, 'Op zoek naar een toekomst. Problematiek van de voormalige Oostbloklanden' *De Architect* special issue 50 1993, pp. 41-51.

Schwartz, Ineke, 'Het bouwbudget als citroen. Rudy Uytenhaak wendt alle mogelijkheden aan voor een optimale architectuur', *Trouw* 14 July 1993.

Sociale woningbouw optimaal benut. Project Weesperstraat, Amsterdam 1993.

Toorn, Roemer van, 'Transparency and autonomous poetry. Recent work by Rudy Uytenhaak', *Archis* no. 8 1993, pp. 17-32.

Versteijlen, Leo, 'Vlakkenbarok. Woningbouw van Rudy Uytenhaak', *De Architect* no. 6 1993, pp. 30-51.

Sources of illustrations

Dienst Ruimtelijke Ordening Amsterdam: p. 75.

Luuk Kramer: p. 52 (above).

Cary Markerink: cover (Koningin Wilhelminaplein), pp. 13, 17, 23, 38 (above), 42, 54, 55 (above), 56, 61 (right above and below), 63, 64, 65 (above), 66, 68, 70, 73, 74, 78, 79 (below) 80, 91 (above), 92 (above), 100 (above), 105 (below), 107 (above), 110, 111 (above), 113 (above and below), 117 (below), 123, 129, 130.

Hans Tulleners: p. 84.

Theo Uytenhaak: p. 116.

Van der Vlugt & Claus: p. 96.

Illustrations not mentioned above have been provided by the architect and his staff, including:

Jérôme Adema, Mariëtte Adriaanssen, Ad van Aert, Hugo Boogaard, John Bosch, Felix Claus, Maurits Cobben, Gé van Dam, Paul van der Erve, Willem Grift, Arie van Harten, Chris Hinderks, André Hoek, Joost Hovenier, Carla Jacobs, Joanne de Jager, Bastiaan Jongerius, Kees Kaan, Joop Klos, Tiemen Koetsier, Gerard Kruunenberg, Freek Meyers, Jasper Molenaar, Harry Pappot, Theo Peppelman, Marco Romano, Tiny Roothans, Jonathan Rose, Jan Schaafsma, Pieter Seeghers, Ria Smit, Kees Stoffels, Onno Vlaanderen, Jan Peter Wingender, Lydia Wullings, Ralph Wyer, Engbert van der Zaag.